The Highly Sensitive Person Real World Guide of Self Discovery

Use Empath & Enneagram To Uncover Your True Personality Type and Learn How To Survive and Thrive in Any Situation

Michael Wilkinson

Copyright © 2018 Michael Wilkinson

All rights reserved.

No part of this publication may be reproduced, stored in a retrieval system, or transmitted, in any form or by any means, electronic, mechanical, photocopying, recording, or otherwise, without the prior written permission of the author and the publishers.

The distribution, uploading, and scanning of this book via the Internet, or via any other means, without the permission of the author is illegal and punishable by law.

Please ensure only authorized electronic editions are purchased, and do not engage in or promote electronic piracy of copyrighted materials.

Disclaimer

This book is not aimed at offering any medical advice or representing medical treatment or advice from your personal healthcare provider. Readers should consult their personal physicians or licensed health professionals concerning their medical conditions and treatments. The author shall not be held responsible or liable for any misuse or misinterpretation of the information provided in this book. The information is not intended for diagnosis, cure or treatment of any ailment.

Be reminded that the author of this book is not a medical professional/doctor/therapist. Only opinions on the basis of personal experiences and research are referenced. The author does not provide any medical advice or prescription of any treatments. Consult your doctor for any medical or health issues.

It is important to note that I research all of the material in my books to bring you the highest quality material. Unfortunately, there are substandard, cheap outsourced books on the non-fiction market nowadays which are developed by different Internet marketing organizations. My aim is to ensure you are provided with only high quality contents as **I do not compromise the high quality of my books**.

Also, if you haven't downloaded your free book already:

The Growth Mindset: How To Become The Best Version of Yourself

To help speed up your personal transformation, I have prepared a special gift for you!

Download my full 88-page e-book "The Growth Mindset: How To Become The Best Version of Yourself"

Visit this Link:

https://www.developsuccessmindset.com/mindset-gift/

Table of Contents

Empath Made Easy 1
Introduction 2
Chapter 1: What it Means to be an Empath 3

   Common Traits 4
   Types of Empaths 6

Chapter 2: Empath Quizzes for the Unsure 9
Chapter 3: How to Embrace Your Gift 12

   It's Not a Curse 13
   Balancing Emotions 15
   Prevent Emotional Drainage 18

Chapter 4: Simple Coping Mechanisms for Any Situation 20
Chapter 5: Even Science Understands Empaths 22

   Emotional Contagion 23
   Electromagnetic Fields 23
   Increased Sensitivity of Dopamine 24
   Synesthesia 24
   Psychologies View 24

Chapter 6: Understanding Energy Effects 26

   Humans and Vibrational Energy 26
   Sensitivity to Energy 27

Chapter 7: A Societal View on Empaths 29
Chapter 8: How to Protect Yourself from Energy Vampires 31

   Identifying Energy Vampires 33
   Protect Yourself 35

Chapter 9: Problems that Empathy can Cause 39
Chapter 10: How to Handle Empathy in Your Life 42

   Relationship Sabotage 43
   Empathy at Work 44

Chapter 11: Become More Self-Aware 46
Chapter 12: Normalizing, Fine Tuning and Maintaining Your Gift 48

   Controlling Emotions 49

Chapter 13: Keeping Out Unwanted Emotions 51
Chapter 14: Healing 55

   Important Truths 60
   Clearing Emotions 61

Chapter 15: How to Support a Young Empath 64
Chapter 16: Exercises You Can do Daily 66
Conclusion 69

Enneagram Made Easy 71
Introduction 72
Part 1: Getting Our Feet Wet, Enneagram Style 73

    Chapter 1: The Enneagram – What Is It and How Do We Use It? 73
        A Brief History of the Enneagram 73
    Chapter 2: The Basic Personality Type 76
        The Nine Types 76
        The Triads 77
        Traps, Avoidances, Idealizations, and Core Beliefs 78
        Vices/Passions 79
        Wings 79
        Levels of Development 80
        Directions of Disintegration (Stress) and Integration (Growth) 80
        Instinctual Variants, a.k.a. "Subtypes" 81
    Chapter 3: What's Your Number? The Type Quiz 83
        Instructions for the Quiz 83
        The Enneagram Type Indicator Quiz 83
        Scoring Your Quiz 87

Part 2: Diving In – Learning About the Types 88

    The Instinctive Triad 88
        Chapter 4: Type 8 – The Challenger 88
        Chapter 5: Type 9 – The Peacemaker 95
        Chapter 6: Type 1 – The Reformer 103
    The Feeling Triad 110
        Chapter 7: Type 2 – The Helper 110
        Chapter 8: Type 3 – The Achiever 118
        Chapter 9: Type 4 – The Individualist 125
    The Thinking Triad 132
        Chapter 10: Type 5 – The Investigator 132
        Chapter 11: Type 6 – The Loyalist 139
        Chapter 12: Type 7 – The Enthusiast 146

Conclusion 153
About The Author 156
Helpful Resources 157
Source Materials 159

Empath Made Easy

How to Thrive in a Chaotic World by Utilizing Your Unique Ability, Developing Your Gift and Mastering Your Personality Using Simple Psychological Tactics for Everyday Use

Introduction

I want to congratulate you on taking all those so important first steps on your journey to self-awareness and love so that you can use your gift to help others and yourself. If you have chosen to purchase this book, I am guessing that you have just realized that you could have the gift of empathy. There are likely a lot of emotions swirling through your mind right now and you could be a little scared. Being scared is normal because you probably don't understand what empathy is. Excitement may also be prevalent because you are ready to take this journey and learn about this new world and everything that it can bring you.

For the most part, empaths who haven't learned how to control their abilities will likely experience a lot of anxiety, nervousness, and maybe even physical pain. When you start feeling the emotions of others so much so that they feel like your own emotions, you can wind up on a rollercoaster of feelings that you can't understand. This book is here to help you come to a place of peace with your ability. You are going to learn exactly what it means to be an empath and why it makes you such a special person.

It's important that you understand you have a lot of power in you. The reason why it has such a deep effect on you is that of how dynamic it is. Being an empath will bring you many gifts and benefits. As you begin to embrace all that you can do, you will notice that opportunities will open up to you that you didn't know were there.

Make sure that you completely absorb and take in every chapter in this book before you continue on. You need to make sure that your spirit is ready for what you are going to learn and unlock with the information found throughout these pages. You will be amazed at the potential that you have living within you.

Chapter 1: What it Means to be an Empath

A simple definition of empathy is having an ability to understand and read people and resonate or to be in tune with others. This can be either voluntary or involuntary. If you are a natural empath, the latter will be true for you.

Empaths are hypersensitive and experience high levels of understanding, compassion, and consideration to others. Their extreme empathy creates something of a tuning fork effect, where they can feel the emotions of the people that they are around. Many empaths are normally unaware of how this works. They have probably accepted the fact that they just feel more sensitive toward certain people.

It doesn't matter whether or not they know it, empaths share many of the same traits that other empaths have.

Being an empath means that you get affected by other people's energy and you have the ability to intuitively feel and perceive others who are around you. Unconsciously, you get influenced by other people's wishes, moods, thoughts, and desires. Being an empath is a lot more than just being super sensitive and it isn't limited to just emotions.

Empaths can perceive spiritual urges and physical sensitivities. They can understand the intentions and motivations of others. A person is either an empath or they aren't. It isn't anything that you can learn. You are open to process other people's energy and feelings. This means you can actually feel, and in many cases, take on the emotions of others. Many empaths will experience things such as unexplained aches and pains, chronic fatigue, or environmental sensitivities each day. All of these can be attributed to outside influences and not so much about yourself. You are basically walking around with a whole lot of accumulated energy, emotions, and karma that has come from others.

Empaths are quiet achievers. They don't like getting compliments because they like to point out other people's achievements. They are very expressive in various areas of emotional connections and they can talk openly and sometimes very frankly. They don't have any problems talking about their feelings as long as someone will listen to them.

They could, however, be the total opposite — reclusive and unresponsive at the best of times. They might sometimes appear to be ignorant. Some have even gotten good at blocking people out and this isn't a bad thing, at least for an empath who is learning and struggling with a huge amount of emotions from others and their own feelings.

Empaths are usually open to feeling what is outside of them more than what they are feeling inside. This means that empaths have a tendency to ignore their own needs. Empaths are usually non-violent, non-aggressive, and most of them are peacemakers. Areas that have a lot of disharmonies can cause empaths to feel very uncomfortable. When they are in the center of a confrontation, empaths will try to settle the situation as quickly as they can, if they don't avoid it completely. If they say something harsh when defending their self, they usually resent their lack of self-control.

Empaths can pick up on other's feelings and project them back without even knowing where they came from. Talking things out is very important for an empath who is learning so they can release emotions. Empaths might develop stronger degrees of knowledge so they can find peace in any given situation.

Empaths can also be very sensitive to videos, movies, news, broadcasts, and television. Violent or emotional dramas that show shocking scenes of pain that were inflicted on children, animals, or adults might bring them to tears.

Empaths might find they like working with people, animals, or nature. They are passionate to help others when they can. They are usually tireless caretakers and teachers for our environment and everything that lives in it.

They can be amazing storytellers because of their ever-expanding knowledge, endless imagination, and inquisitive minds. They are extremely gentle and old romantics at heart. They are usually the "keepers of family history and ancestral knowledge." If they aren't obvious family historians, they are usually the ones who listen to stories that have been passed down and they possess most of the family's history.

They might have a broad interest in music that suits all of their temperaments. The people who are closest to them might question how they can listen to a certain type of music and then a few minutes later, they have changed to something completely different. Song lyrics could have powerful effects on empaths, especially if it is relevant to things they are or have experienced.

Common Traits

While every empath is a little different, they do share some common traits that can be easily spotted.

1. Many are introverted

Crowds usually overwhelm them as it amplifies their empathy. They like to have one-on-one contact with people or little groups. Even if they are a bit more extroverted, they still try to limit the amount of time they spend at parties or in crowds.

2. Highly Sensitive

Empaths are great listeners. They give naturally. They are open spiritually. If you need someone with heart, you need to find an empath. These nurturers will help you no matter what. Their feelings can be easily hurt. Most empaths have been told they need to "toughen up" or are just "too sensitive."

3. Highly Intuitive

Empaths experience the world through their intuition. This is a skill they have to develop so they can learn how to listen to their gut feelings about others. This helps them stay away from negative people and find relationships that are positive.

4. They absorb emotions

They are very in tune with the moods of others, whether they be good or bad. They sometimes feel everything at extremes. They will consume negative emotions. This causes them to become exhausted. When surrounded with love, their bodies will flourish.

5. Intimate relationships can become overwhelming

Being together a lot can be hard on empaths and they might steer away from being intimate with others. Deep down, they are afraid of losing their identity. For an empath to feel at ease in their relationship, their normal paradigm needs to be redefined.

6. Nature replenishes empaths

Everyday life can be hard on an empath. Nature can help nourish and restore them. It helps them release their burdens. They take refuge in the presence of bodies of water especially the ocean and green things in nature.

7. Alone time

Because of their heightened senses, empaths find it to be draining when they are around a lot of people. They need to have some alone time in order to recharge themselves. Just a short escape will keep them from having an emotional overload. One good example is that empaths will often choose to drive themselves places so that they will be able to leave whenever.

8. Energy vampire targets

Their sensitivity can make them an easy mark for energy vampires. These people will do more damage than just damaging their physical energy. Narcissists are very dangerous and could make their victim feel as if they are unlovable.

9. Tuned senses

Empaths might find their nerves are easily frazzled by excessive talking noise or smells.

10. They just know

Empaths know things without being told. This is a knowing that is more than intuition or gut feelings. They might describe their understanding in this way.

11. Sometimes gives too much

Empaths have big hearts and they will try to help other people's pain. It is natural for them to reach out to those who are in need and try to ease their suffering. Unfortunately, empaths don't stop with just that. Instead, they consume their problems and feel upset and completely drained.

12. Addictive personality

Empaths will sometimes turn to drugs, sex, alcohol, or other addictions in order to block out emotions. This is their form of self-protection to help them hide from others and things.

13. Easily distracted

School, work, and their home life need to be interesting otherwise they will switch off and just start to daydream or doodle.

14. Drawn to metaphysical and holistic things

Even though many empaths love to heal others, they will turn away from being a healer even after they have been qualified because they will take on too many emotions from their patients. This will happen more if they don't actually know they are an empath. Empaths are open to things that others consider unthinkable. They don't get surprised or shocked easily.

15. Low back problems and digestive disorders

The solar plexus chakra is in the middle of the stomach and is the seat of emotions. This is where empaths will feel other people's emotions and this causes this area to weaken. This can lead to anything from stomach ulcers to IBS. Low back problems could happen if they are ungrounded, along with other problems. A person who doesn't know they are an empath will always be ungrounded.

16. They can read honesty

If they have a loved one or friend lying to them, they will know it instantly. Many empaths will try not to focus on this fact because they get hurt knowing a person close to them is lying to them.

Types of Empaths

Many people don't realize there are different types of empaths. If you're an empath, it is important that you know which one you are so you can make the most of your gift and can take care of yourself.

1. Physical or Medical Empath

These empaths can pick up on the bodily energy of the people they are with. They can instantly tell what is bothering another person. Many people who have this type of empathy will be a healer either in the alternative or conventional sense. They might feel awareness in the body when they treat someone else. They might notice blockages in someone's energy that should be treated.

A medical empath will notice symptoms in others and might feel these same symptoms in their own body. Once they take on the physical symptoms of others, this could lead to other health problems. People who have chronic illnesses such as fibromyalgia or an autoimmune disease might find it to be helpful to strengthen their energy field so they can turn off their abilities when they need to. If you can train yourself in a specific type of healing, it might help you strengthen this ability.

2. Emotional Empath

This is the most common type of empath. These empaths will pick up people's emotions easily when they are around others and they take on the emotions like they were their own. They experience other people's feelings deeply in their own body. For example, emotional empaths can become extremely sad around people who are experiencing sadness.

It's important for an emotional empath to be able to tell the difference between their emotions and the emotions of the people they are near. Once they can do this, they can help people without completely draining themselves.

3. Plant Empath

These empaths can intuitively know what a plant needs. They have a green thumb and are gifted for putting the right plants in the right places in their homes or garden. Many will work in wild landscapes, gardens, or parks where they can use their gift for the greater good. In fact, if you are in an occupation that involves plants, there is a good chance that you are a plant empath. Many people will receive guidance from plants or trees by hearing what is in their mind.

If you are a plant empath, you know that you need a lot of contact with trees and plants. You could strengthen this bond by sitting quietly near a special tree or plant and tuning into it to see if it needs anything.

4. Geomantic Empath

This type of empathy is often referred to as environmental or place empathy. These empaths are closely connected to the physical landscape. If you feel uncomfortable or very happy in various situations or environments, you might be a geomantic empath.

These empaths will feel deep connections to various places. They might be pulled to groves, churches, sacred stones, or other areas with lots of power. They might also be able to pick up the history of places and might feel the sadness, joy, or fear that could have happened in that area many years ago. They are very connected with the natural world and hurt deeply when it gets damaged.

This empath needs to spend a lot of time in nature. They might also find it healing to help on any projects that help the environment. It is important to create beautiful and harmonious surroundings for your everyday life. They will feel happier if their house is full of natural plants and smells.

5. Claircognizant or Intuitive Empath

This empath will get information from others just by being near them. Just a glance will give them all sorts of insights. They will know if other people are lying just because they can sense these intentions. People who have this gift will resonate with other people's energetic fields and will be able to read their energy.

People who have this ability should surround themselves with people who they are aligned with. They might have to strengthen their own energetic field. This will ensure that they don't get bombarded with thoughts and emotions of others.

6. Animal Empath

The majority of empaths will experience a connection to animals, but an animal empath might devote their entire life to caring for our furry little friends. People who have this particular gift understand the needs of an animal and some might even be able to communicate with them.

If this is your empathy type, you are probably surrounded by animals already. The study of the psychology or biology of animals may help you to improve your talents. You might even consider becoming an animal healer because your talent might help you to figure out what ails them.

Chapter 2: Empath Quizzes for the Unsure

You might be wondering if there is a way to know for certain if you are an empath or not. It is more up to you to understand yourself and figure out if you are one or not. There is a test to help you determine if you are an empath or not.

Chances are if you have ever felt another person's pain or felt the energy in a room change without understanding what happened, you are probably an empath. We're going to see how much of the following you can connect with.

For every statement, give it a "3" for always, "2" for sometimes, and "0" for never.

1. You begin to feel drained when you are near certain people.
2. You can sense when others are in pain or sad.
3. You experience intense negative or positive impressions when you first meet a person and it ends up being correct.
4. You immediately know when somebody says one thing but means something else.
5. Most people don't understand how deeply you feel and why you can't let things go.
6. When you witness something sad such as an animal being abused, it takes you a long time to stop feeling upset about it.
7. You sometimes feel like you can feel the entire world's pain.
8. You can't watch sad or violent movies or read the news because it upsets you too much or it makes you feel sick.
9. You feel as if you look at life from a perspective different than everyone else. It feels almost like you're the only one.
10. You have days where you become so overwhelmed by the pain in the world that you would rather just hide out at home than face anybody.
11. You feel sick or in pain when you are around specific people for no physical reason or you feel as if you take on another people's symptoms and feelings.
12. You constantly feel the exact same sensations when you are near certain people. Each time you are with a specific friend, you might feel mad for no reason
13. You walk into a place and feel different energy without understanding the reason for it. For example, you walk into your office and get hit with sensations of frustration.
14. You feel like your mood changes when specific people come into a room.
15. You feel like your mood changes quickly but you don't know why.

16. You get overwhelmed when there are many people around but you don't understand why you are feeling overwhelmed.

17. People get pulled to you and want a "fix" to make them happy. You may even find that children and pets are pulled towards you.

18. People look at you as their "energy source" since you can brighten their day or you help their emotions.

19. Walking through nature is the only thing that makes you feel good.

20. You like being near water, especially when you feel overwhelmed.

21. You have a tendency to care about those around you instead of caring about yourself and you feel as if you must help everyone else, even if you are feeling burned out.

22. People ask you why you are "a bleeding heart" or they make fun of you because you feel things very deeply.

23. You have times in your life where you went through traumatic times and you felt completely numb.

24. You understand that animals and plants have awareness or souls and you can feel their emotions.

25. You have a hard time taking care of yourself since you always take care of others.

Now take a few minutes to add up your scores.

If you scored between zero and 25:

You do have some traits of an empath, but you aren't considered to be one. It is important that you make sure you are taken care of and be sure not to get overwhelmed. There is a chance you already have a decent balance between setting boundaries and helping others.

If you scored between 25 and 50:

You're an empath. You can feel things a bit differently than a normal person. You don't just relate to a person's feelings, you feel them like they're yours. You might feel exhausted a lot and don't understand why, since you don't know, you give out too much energy and you take in a lot of negativity. You may be balanced. There isn't any doubt that you are going to benefit from different resources that will help you with the new found power.

If you scored between 50 and 75:

If you are in this range, you are known as an extreme empath. You soak in others' emotions without knowing you are doing so. You can feel the energy of the room without having any visual cues. With a score this high, you are very open to suffering and pain in the world. You will get too overwhelmed by doing too much. If you don't work on your traits, you might wind up getting very sick.

Chapter 3: How to Embrace Your Gift

Once you have come to the realization that you are in fact an empath, it will be like somebody has removed a blindfold. All of a sudden things will make sense. Your feelings, interactions, experiences, and thoughts with others will be understood and seen against your personality type.

Labels have been thrown at you your entire life. You were likely called troubled, sensitive, or weak. Now you have discovered a label that fits perfectly. This is going to be the best feeling in the world. You have found a new identity, a sense of self, and a belief that you can explore your inner and outer workings with more confidence and knowledge.

After you understand that you're an empath, you won't feel alone. You will get to join a unified collection of others that share your gift. You will be filled with knowing you belong. This is likely something that you haven't gotten to experience in some time. You start to scour the internet trying to find places that empaths go such as forums, blogs, support groups, and Facebook. You will feel thrilled once you find them. There aren't just a couple of options either. You will find literally thousands of empaths.

Once you have come to understand that you are an empath, the words you know will expand. You will start talking about vibrations, lightworker, shielding, intuitive empath, grounding, and much more. This will all become normal for you.

You will begin to learn more about what empaths can do for the world, what challenges they have to face, and opportunities that come to them due to their abilities. While you work to research your new skills, you will shed some light on things that have happened to you in your past. Feeling a good or bad vibe when you meet a person without speaking to them, you now understand. You will now understand why you don't like getting bad news or being stuck in crowded places.

After you know that you are an empath, you will understand why everybody likes to come to you with all of their problems. You have always been the perfect listener and everybody is able to tell that, even if they don't know why.

For your entire life, you have been the person that your friends came to when they needed a shoulder to cry on. Up until now, it has probably felt like a burden, but now you understand. You start to realize that you have the talent of being able to see through another's eyes, walking in their shoes, and feeling how they feel. This means that you have taken in their sadness and despair while you were helping them to work through their feelings. You now have a good understanding of why this happened.

Once you have realized you are an empath, you will be able to learn how to handle your abilities. Just the ability to identify as one will allow you to find help for problems that you have been going through. The tool chest you have that was empty is now filling up as you become more confident about embracing the world around you.

You no longer have to be shy and fearful of the feelings of people, sensations, and places. You will likely not feel completely relaxed when you're outside of your comfort zone, but you will be willing to head outside of your comfort zone from time to time.

Once you know you are an empath, you will start to recognize that this is who you are and you are always going to be like this. You will learn how to change and grow with time, but the truth is that you are always going to be an empath. This can be a little bit disheartening and a lot liberating.

You now understand your essence and you will be able to quit trying to figure out ways to silence your natural tendencies. You will accept yourself and show those around your true self.

You will also have to deal with the struggles you will have to face. This is never going to stop. You will become better at coping but there are going to be times when your mind is going to cause feelings of sorrow and sadness.

Once you know you're an empath, you will notice your world has changed forever. You will have more explanations for things and you will understand more of who you are. You will be able to enter into a new chapter in your life. You will be reborn into a new you, one where you no longer feel lost. You will discover your true self. You will be able to celebrate your wholeness.

It's Not a Curse

You are likely very sick of hearing people tell you that your sensitivities make you weak. Those sensitivities are exactly what allow you to experience life at different depths. Sensitivity is what allows you to listen to your needs and dreams. Sensitivity allows you to help those around you. Sensitivity will let see the divinity of life and its beauty.

An untrained empath will likely be in constant pain due to their abilities. Your emotions will be a constant roller coaster and you will likely stay confused. This doesn't have to be the case.

Once you have learned how to surrender, observe, accept, and release, it will turn into just another aspect of you. The word soar in a simple definition means "to fly or transcend." This means that you will be able to learn how to soar over all the emotional darkness and congestion while you live your life as you.

Let's take a look at how you can SOAR:

- Surrender – first you have to learn how to relax your whole body. Take a deep breath in. Surrender any tension or discomfort that you may feel. Make sure you don't fight this. Feel all of the emotions that you are holding in. Before you surrender them, make sure you identify what the feelings are.

- Observe – allow yourself to feel your emotions. Do not judge them. How do they sound, smell, look like, and taste? Make sure you use all of your sense to create an image of them. The anxiety inside could feel like slime that squishes to your core. If all of your energy is clashing, it could feel as if you have a raging fire inside of you. Remember that you need to observe these and don't allow them to attack you. This is going to be a lot easier said than done. Allow the feelings to rise up and flow, just like an ocean tide.

- Accept – as you observe the emotions and sensations that are in you, accept them. Do not resist them. Welcome them in as a temporary visitor. They are going to leave. Nothing is going to remain forever.

- Release – as you are going through the motions of the past steps, you will start to feel these emotions slip away. Extremely intense and repressed emotions could end up rearing their ugly heads. Don't let these worry you. Carefully go through all of the steps as often as you have to so that you can get rid of them

You should practice this technique like a meditation. Set aside a few minutes every day to relax and calm yourself. There are lots of different ways that you can do this such as listening to calming music, walking barefooted outside, humming, focusing on your breath, and visualizing.

You are basically learning how to self-soothe. Figure out a practice that will work for you. If you aren't able to center yourself, you won't be able to succeed with the practice that is coming up.

To help you out, here is a sample grounding process:

You may notice that you are feeling anxious or sick. A lot of people are around you that could be sending out bad vibes, are demanding, laughing, gossiping, or just being loud. You must take a break. You are getting ready to take a break. This is the time for you to center and focus.

You are taking your lunch break. You start to feel tired and you are filled with an angry and impatient energy. If you can, sit outside on the Earth. Take in a few deep breaths. Notice the ground under you. Feel how the wind touches your face. You can center yourself in nature more easily.

Sit very still and breathe for a full ten minutes. If you have to, set a timer. You have started to feel grounded but you are still holding in restlessness. It tastes bad and appears to you like a storm cloud. Watch it. Let it be there. It could manifest in your stomach, shoulders, or neck. Let it be and watch. You remain grounded in nature. Watch and accept. It is there, so don't fight it.

Let a few more minutes pass. Shift your focus to how you feel and consciously experience your emotions. Be present with the uncomfortable sensations. Notice how it starts to slip away. Notice as it leaves your body and meets your consciousness. Watch it fade away.

Bring yourself back to the present and understand that your negative feeling has gone.

You will have to experiment with the procedure. You must make it work for you. This procedure is here to help you create mindfulness without experiencing attachment or resistance. You mustn't be rigid when you follow this. Allow it to naturally flow. If you meet an emotion with acceptance and no attachment, it is going to slip away. Empaths tend to suffer because they are unconsciously attacked by things around them.

Balancing Emotions

Being an empath can be challenging but it can also provide benefits to you and those around you. In order for you to experience the benefits, you will have to understand how to make it work so that you don't become a victim to the emotions of other people. Here's how:

- You are first

This tends to go against everything that has been ingrained in your brain. When you make sure that your needs have been met, you will be able to take care of those around you better. Empathy works best when you aren't depleted.

You must make sure that you are taken care of all the time. If you aren't, you are going to find that you are filled with the needs of others. Figure out things that will allow you to be a better you:

- o Meditate

- o Become a pen pal
- o Learn yoga
- o Get lots of sleep
- o Take an art class
- o Make dinner for a loved one
- o Exercise
- Set up boundaries

You can only function with so many thoughts and feelings in your head and heart. You need to limit what you take in from others. You have to accept the fact that you are only human and you can't help everybody.

If a person needs to talk with you about something in their life, set a time limit. This isn't because of a lack of love. This is so that you can support them the best way you can. If you allow yourself to be exhausted physically or emotionally, you are going to shut down and your empathy will lack.

Be conscious of all the information that you consume. The world is full of lots of happiness. But there is also a lot of sadness and injustice. Do your best to avoid an emotional rollercoaster. Limit the time you spend on social media or watching the news. As an empath, you can get caught up in the stories of others and you will forget to take care of your emotions. This can happen even if you don't know the person all that well.

- Release everything

It's amazing when we are able to celebrate with others. As an empath, you will feel what others feel. You will experience the joys of a child, wedding, and promotion. You also feel hopeless when you hear about somebody else's loses like losing a loved one, being diagnosed with cancer, or a rough breakup.

This is where separation can help. The fact of the matter is you didn't break up with anybody, you aren't fighting a disease, and nobody in your family has passed away. When your friends are around, you show them acceptance by letting them know that you love them. It's important that you understand that you don't have to embrace or keep their situation.

Feel it and let it go. Figure out how you can release a person's emotions. Find a person who can help you release these emotions. Since they aren't close to the situation, they won't hold onto it and they will help you. You have to deal with your own hurt. You don't have to help everybody else as well.

- Process emotions

The majority of empaths can sympathize with other people but they will neglect their needs. They become numb to their needs from all of the emotions they feel from others. This has to stop so that you can process your emotions.

Nobody has to be an island. Just because those around you bring in their feelings and thoughts doesn't mean you must rely only on yourself. Everybody needs some sort of guide to help them. Emotions can be handled formally or informally. The important thing is that you practice it regularly. Try:

- Go to lunch with your best friend once a week.
- Keep a journal.
- Process your emotions with somebody before bed.
- Talk to a spiritual leader.
- Go to a trained therapist.
- Find a life coach.
- Go to group counseling.

- Celebrate

As an empath, you know how to experience pain and joy. You will notice that pain is what likes to stick to you and will weigh you down. When you feel these negative emotions, it's important that you learn how to be emotionally balanced. Carrying the pain of others isn't helpful.

Celebration is a great way to bring positive rhythms into your life. It doesn't matter what is going on in your life, you can always celebrate. Try a few of these:

- Throw a party because you dropped a pound.
- Spend time with your kids.
- Take yourself on a date.
- Take a co-worker to dinner to celebrate their promotion.
- Give your partner a gift just because.

Empathy is a great way to allow others to know they feel connected and understood. Don't let yourself get exhausted. You need a balanced life so that you don't experience resentment. Let it empower others, but put yourself first.

Prevent Emotional Drainage

It can be overwhelming to have other's emotions constantly bombarding you. Empaths bring light and love along with their compassion. Experiencing the emotions of others comes with downsides. All of the negativity can deplete you. Other people will sometimes take advantage of you. To make sure that you thrive, it's important that your energy is protected. This is the only way that you can make sure that you can take care of others.

The following six ways can up your powers without being depleted by other's emotions:

1. Alone time

It's important for empaths to find alone time to get away from the negativity, drama, and stress of the world. If you don't take time alone, you will likely start feeling overwhelmed. You should make it a priority to find some alone time and use this time to whatever it takes to stay balanced and healthy. Writing in a journal, taking a walk outside, or meditation can help you to work through your own emotions.

2. Create an energy space

This is a space that will restore you. You should try to find a calm and peaceful space where you can't be distracted by the outside world. Some people will create a space in nature or in an empty space in their house. You could even lock yourself in your bathroom if you have to. Your space should be beautiful and full of candles, places, or artwork. Find stuff that puts you in a state of calm. That space should not be cluttered or untidy. The cleanliness will put your mind at ease. Essential oil or incense can help to improve the calmness.

3. Protection from negativity

You have to make sure that you protect yourself from negativity when you can. Limit the time that you spend with negative, toxic, and critical people. You need to find the time to restore when you have been around them. Avoid negative media and focus on positive things. Fill your world with inspiring things and quit allowing yourself to be pulled into other's negativity. Visualizing a ball of gold light wrapping itself around you when you notice you are being pulled into negativity is a great practice. This allows negativity to bounce off of you instead of you absorbing it.

4. Remove negative energy

It doesn't matter how great you are at protecting yourself, you will pick up bad emotions. You could find yourself stuck in bad thinking patterns. Empaths aren't able to be upbeat and positive all the time. The grief of the world will often bring you down into depression. You don't have to think of these emotions as negative. Grief and sadness are perfectly normal. If you deny this, it isn't going to go away. You need to feel these emotions completely and allow them to disappear. You should dance, exercise, and journal to help process the negativity.

5. Help the world with your ability

Empaths understand that problems won't be solved with hate or rejections. Instead, you have to solve them with love and understanding. Make use of your energy in a positive way to help others. It could be small things like cleaning up litter or donating some time at a food bank. Doing something good will help you to remain positive about being an empath instead of feeling as if it is a burden.

6. Chase your dreams

Empaths will often neglect their dreams because they remain sensitive to the needs of others. You need to remember that you are a unique human being. You were placed on earth for a reason. Don't allow other people to take all of your energy so that you don't have enough to follow your dreams.

Make sure that you take the time to follow your desires and make them something sacred. If you don't make a conscious effort and decision on how you are going to spend your energy, others are going to spend it on what they want. You will end up missing your purpose.

Empathy is a true gift. Being sensitive needs to be managed in order to make sure that you have the energy to live. Take some time to support you. This isn't selfish, it's necessary. This is the only way you can successfully share your gift with the world.

Chapter 4: Simple Coping Mechanisms for Any Situation

There are a lot of techniques in this book that can help you stay balanced and grounded, but sometimes you need something that you can access quickly. The following coping mechanisms can help you out when you are faced with a tough or stressful situation.

1. Water

The body is 75% water and a lot of body tissue is 95% water, so it shouldn't be a surprise that water is the top at the self-healing list. A lot of people aren't aware of the fact that they are dehydrated. Not enough water will create issues with how your physical and energetic bodies function. It also affects your general wellbeing and advances the aging process.

Water is a great protector for empaths and it's important that they have a lot of it inside and outside of their body. Most should aim for eight glasses of water each day to replenish what you naturally excrete through sweating, urination, and so on. The heavier you are, the more you should drink.

Water can also wash away things. Washing in water is not only good for your hygiene. Water is also able to cleanse your energetic body and remove negativity. When you find yourself in an emotional situation, grab a glass of water.

2. Create a shield

There are going to be situations that you rather avoid, but you can't because of the significance in your life. Important work functions, family get-togethers, and social events could involve energies that you find hard to deal with.

You will have to find a way to cope with these circumstances. To do this, you can create a mental barrier that will allow you to control what comes through and deflect the negativity. Imagine that you have a golden bubble surrounding you. Here you can focus inwards and find a balance with the troubles on the outside. When your energy starts to drain, you have the bubble to retreat inside of to stop the flow.

3. Repeat affirmations

Empaths tend to be open and giving people but this doesn't mean they are always positive. To remain positive even in negative situations, it's a good idea to have some positive affirmations that you can repeat to yourself to push away the negativity. Try this one the next time you are feeling down: "When I am with draining people, I will protect my own energy. I will create good boundaries. I will tell people 'no' when it is right. I will strengthen my relationships that serve a positive purpose."

4. Switch up your views

As an empath, it can be frustrating to interact with others. You have a higher ability when it comes to being kind and caring for people and when you notice others being harmed in any way, it hurts.

Because of this, it's a good idea to get out of your mind and watch the other person not as evil or bad, but as hurting or misguided. Most of the time, people who act opposite to you, do so because of how they were brought up or some form of trauma. They probably have a hard time envisioning the world the way you see it, so they don't act as you do.

When you change your perspective, you will reduce how they hurt you. You might even find some sympathy and love for them instead of frustration and bewilderment.

Chapter 5: Even Science Understands Empaths

Many things in life might appear to be magic until we can figure out how they work and understand the process involved. Unfortunately, the discovery for empaths is still being done. There has been a research done on mirror neurons and it is placing some light on the possible explanation for why empaths can experience other people's emotions.

Mirror neurons are thought to be a neurophysiological mechanism involved in how we understand other people's actions and learn to imitate them. There were first studies in the context of motor skills and they found that they fired up when a monkey watched another person perform a certain action. This brought them to a hypothesis that watching someone will trigger an internal response to help us imitate and mimic what we see. The act of watching another person experience something activates the neurons in our brain even when we don't actually perform this action. (Acharya & Shukla, 2012)

Marco Iacoboni introduced that mirror neuron might have the potential physiological basis for empathy and morality since they are involved in the way we perceive and interpret the experiences of those around us. In their simplest form, these neurons are triggered through observation of a physical gesture in another person that fires the same neurons in the person observing. What is amazing about this is that it happens consistently even though the person observing isn't moving anything. It works only on an internal representation of the actions and not a physical limitation.

For example, at a baseball game, neurons that get activated by the catcher when he catches the ball are also fired in the audience. This same process is also working when we watch somebody experience some form of physical pain or if we notice a certain facial expression of anger or worry. Our brain can interpret the meaning of these situations by experiencing them internally through its own mirror neurons. There are many ways to trigger mirror neurons — seeing a ball gets kicked, hearing the sound the ball makes when it gets kicked, or say the word kick could cause your mirror neurons to get fired up.

The firing pattern of mirror neurons is very sophisticated. In fact, the pattern is dependent on the meaning or context of the action that is observed like raising your hand to grab a ball or raising your hand if you have a question. Both actions involve the same muscles but they don't have the same intentions, so they trigger different mirror neuron pathways.

This is why Iacoboni believed that the firing patterns of these neurons are complex enough that it will let people know the intent of another person depending on the action's context. The presence of the process is important when you begin to think about how relating and understanding other people are important in our ability to survive in society. This gets supported by different bodies of research on the process known as emotional contagion. (Iacoboni, 2009)

Emotional Contagion

This is a process where a group or a single person influences the behavior of other people or groups through either an unconscious or conscious induction of behavioral attitudes and emotional states. This is a process that has deep roots in the human psyche. Studies show that newborns will imitate the facial expressions of other people within a few minutes of being born.

Even adults tend to imitate other people's demeanor, often unconsciously. This mimicry causes emotions from one to another and plays a big role in our social relationships. In fact, people are more likely to like a person that imitates them. It is thought that mimicry can make us feel more connected to others. It also gives us a positive emotional experience. This emotional contagion comes from basic mimicry as we work to feel loved by those who are around us. From birth, we spontaneously register and try to reproduce non-verbal language.

Even though science has ventured quite far, the empath experience seems to indicate that there is a human process where humans can innately sense other people's emotions in ways that aren't completely controlled by their conscious mind. Empaths wouldn't mind being able to turn off this every now and then so they can feel their own emotions. However, this experience is unconscious and uncontrollable. Most empaths have reported feeling overwhelmed by other's emotions without wanting to experience them. (Barsade, 2002)

Typically, when someone wants to improve a skill they make a conscious decision to do so and this gets followed by some sort of practice program and learning experience. There are some who are better at this than others so their need to practice might be shorter. For empaths, the physical manifestation happens first. They begin to feel what other people feel and they don't even realize what is going on. It is only after this has happened that they begin to embark on their quest to understand what is happening. Many empaths first thought is "How do I stop this?"

Being an empath never presents itself as a learned skill. It isn't something that a child can wish to have and then develop with practice. The initial trigger is usually a physiological one that leads to an emotional experience and then to conscious awareness. They will feel first then understand their gift later. Most say they don't have any control over the process. This means empathy is an innate ability and not everyone will experience this. Very little of the population will have this ability. Everyone can perceive a person's emotions. Only empaths have the unusual sensitivity to feel emotional cues.

Electromagnetic Fields

This finding is based on the fact that the heart and brain generate an electromagnetic field. According to HeartMath Institute, these fields send information about a person's emotions and thoughts. Empaths are particularly sensitive to this input and are usually overwhelmed by it. They have stronger emotional and physical responses to changes within the electromagnetic fields of the sun and earth. Empaths understand that everything that happens to the sun and earth will have an impact on their energy and state of mind. (McCraty, Atkinson, Tomasino, & Tiller, 1998)

Increased Sensitivity of Dopamine

Dopamine is a neurotransmitter that increases the activity of neurons and is connected to the pleasure response. Research shows that introverted empaths are typically more sensitive to dopamine than extroverts. This means they require less dopamine to be happy. This might explain why they are more content with meditation, reading, and alone time. They don't need external stimulation from social gatherings. Extroverts need a dopamine rush from those types of events. They can't seem to get enough of it.

Synesthesia

Synesthesia is a neurological condition where two senses are paired in the brain. For example, a person can see when they hear a specific piece of music or they taste words. Some famous synesthetics include Billy Joel, violinist Itzhak Perlman, and Isaac Newton. However, when it comes to mirror-touch synesthesia, people can feel the sensations and emotions of others in their body as if it were their own pain.

Psychologies View

Psychology has used the term empathy for a long time to describe a person's ability to see what other people might be feeling. This is also known as "walking in someone else's shoes." Empathy plays an important part in our social interactions. Empathy can affect how we act toward other people. It works like a glue that holds humans together.

Theodore Lipps has always been considered to be the father of the term empathy. He described it as how we perceived the mental state of those around us through a process of inner imitation. The process involves different areas in the brain like the endocrine system, hypothalamic-pituitary-adrenal axis, autonomic nervous system, and the cortex.

Even though people who have some psychopathologies like sociopaths can exhibit a lack of empathy, this skill has a strong biological foundation. Babies can recognize different types of emotions at a very young age and toddlers can develop empathy as they grow. Young children can identify the emotions of other people as well as interpret them correctly.

Recent studies have described two different systems that are involved in psychological empathy — an emotion-based contagion and a cognitive perspective-taking system. Emotional empathy seems to activate what is known as the inferior frontal gyrus. Cognitive empathy is more tied to the motor mirror neuron system. Rogers' model of empaths is closer to cognitive empathy than emotional empathy. (Riess, 2017)

Psychological experiments that study empathy will often use observation in order to trigger a person's empathic response. They will have the empath watch someone who is placed in a situation that is supposed to elicit strong emotions.

Rogers says that empathy involves an "as if" condition. A person could experience empathy when they can imagine what another person feels. This isn't any different than what empaths experience. Empaths feel things as their very own. It isn't something that is imagined or coming from external stimuli.

Chapter 6: Understanding Energy Effects

Energy or Universal Energy is the very basis of human existence. The electricity that gives power to your home, the gas that fuels your car, the sun that warms your body, are all forms of that energy.

Universal energy sustains all life and brings important energy to all things that live. The entire Universe, beginning with the stars to the little atoms that make them, as well as the world and human bodies, everything that we do or say is full of Universal energy at its core.

While we might see the world and everything that is in it as something physical or material, Quantum Physics thinks that everything exists was created by this energy that continuously flows and can change forms. Even Nobel Prize-winning scientists have proven this fact. Since we are normally viewing ourselves and the tangible things that are around us, it is hard to accept things as just energy.

These scientists have found that our "reality" is made up of atoms. There are millions of small vortexes of energy that vibrates and spins. They look like teeny, tiny tornadoes. Whether we see things as a solid, gas, or liquid all depends on the speed that the atoms move at.

Humans and Vibrational Energy

Since energy gives everything a vibration that decides its nature and the things it created, all humans have a vibration. The physical phenomenon of vibration and the spiritual vibration that we have inside us are different things.

The best capacity and power that man has is being able to receive and express thoughts. These thoughts are a combined form of this universal energy directed and created by a certain entity.

When trying to explain a thought, it's important to explain that the person who came up with it must be in control, but very few people are successful at doing just that. A thought, therefore, is a compact form of energetic manifestation. (Brown, et al., 2014)

The energy that vibrates on the low end of the spectrum moves slowly and tends to be dense and tangible. The human form tends to have slow wavelengths, in the scheme of the universe. Since we are a lower frequency, we view our selves as tangible and physical beings.

People feel that they are separate from everything and everyone because their energy vibrates at different frequencies from the things that exist around them. However, we are intrinsically connected to everything around us because our energy communicates, absorbs, interlocks, connects, and interacts with the other energy.

Sensitivity to Energy

There are those who are more in tune with the vibrations of the universal. They typically feel the environment's energy and even the energy of people that they aren't related to.

As the planet's vibration grows, more and more people are becoming receptive to this Universal energy surrounding all of us. The following signs will let you know if you are more sensitive to the world's energy.

1. You can feel the cycles of the moon

Every month of the year, the moon cycles from New to Full. The moon phases represent different emotions. Sensitive souls have a tendency to be extremely synchronized with these lunar phases.

While full, empaths will often feel a desire to end something in their life. There are some empaths who will find it hard to understand the power that the moon has over them. This will sometimes cause them to feel off during specific times.

2. Feel uncomfortable in crowded areas

Empaths will feel very overwhelmed and angry when in crowded spaces or public places. The reason for this is due to the fact that they can feel the energy of those who are around them.

Sensitive people and empaths have a tendency to notice their environment more and this includes certain smells, lights, and sounds that could end up becoming overwhelming. This becomes too difficult for them to fix, which is why they need to learn how to protect themselves.

3. Their intuition is on point

Empaths are extremely conscious of their environment, the energy of those around them, and this makes their intuition strong. They will end up knowing things before it happens or they are able to feel when a close friend is going through a rough patch.

4. They seek spiritual connections

Those who have more sensitivity to energy will have deeper desires to connect with somebody on a spiritual level, create a spiritual family, or a home that they are able to deeply resonate with.

5. Extreme dreams

Empaths tend to have vivid and intense dreams that are creative, which they will remember in great detail. For these people, dreaming becomes a chance to experience places and dimensions and explore different levels of reality.

6. Spiritual development

Because they are so creative, empaths yearn to learn about what their soul needs. Empaths are willingly open to every moment so that they can view the world from different perspectives. They will usually experience a spiritual awakening through things like opening their third eye and accessing their Kundalini energy.

7. They want to find purpose

For empaths, their life isn't just about simple pleasures, material security, family, or work. They feel like their life is deeper and bigger. They will spend much of their time trying to find their real purpose

Empaths want to be a positive impact on the world and they will try to make a personal contribution. Since that will often become their focus, they may end up feeling disappointed by people who don't share their same viewpoint.

Chapter 7: A Societal View on Empaths

When talking about living as an empath, there are two ways that things could go. Society will either support you, is interested in your gifts, and love you for it, OR they think there is something seriously wrong with you, you are too sensitive, or melodramatic.

It is great when society is supportive, but how many times have you ever been called these things: melodramatic, temperamental, weak, fragile, wussy, feeble, wimpy, thin-skinned, spineless, or overly sensitive. This is something that most empaths have to face.

Empaths can happen in an estimated five percent of the population. The ability that

empaths possess is both a blessing and a curse. They can become amazing listeners and counselors. They know how to comfort people and they will assist the people around them. They find these jobs painful and tiring and it is worse when people don't understand them or just write them off as "weird."

Most of society will tend to be more open to empaths now than in the past. More empaths are cherished for their wonderful gift. They are still faced with a lot of misguided perceptions. Let's look at some of these societal myths and debunk them.

1. Empaths are psychologically frail.

The truth is, they are biologically programmed to be sensitive and to be in tune with their environment.

Empaths walk around with the entire world's accumulated problems and this can cause inner emotional tension for them. This is why they are more prone to showing signs of "weakness" and crying.

Empaths also find it hard to take part in normal activities. They feel emotions more deeply than others, which mean they are viewed as "weak minded", "wussy", or "frail."

2. Empaths are self-absorbed and navel-gazing.

Empaths focus more on others than themselves. Empaths are unexplainably moody and quiet on the outside at times. The reason for this has nothing to do with them being self-absorbed. Instead, they are deeply affected by the exterior emotions of those around them that they feel like their own.

3. Empaths are lazy.

Truth is, they lack physical, emotional, and mental energy because of their intense empathic abilities to understand other people.

Empaths have been diagnosed with headaches, insomnia, fibromyalgia, and chronic fatigue syndrome. When their body is continuously overloaded with stress, pressure, and tension, it gets translated into their body. This will often result in some form of illness. When they lack energy, they will often prefer to relax instead, but this in no way makes them lazy.

4. Empaths are mentally ill.

The truth is, they are magnets of negative energy. This will cause them to have a psychological imbalance.

Empaths are great listeners, counselors, and confidants. Because of this, people are drawn to their caring natures just like a magnet. This means that empaths are going to experience a lot of emotional dumping from others. They will sometimes have a hard time releasing all that negative energy.

Unfortunately, this will cause them to have lingering depressive feelings. This means empaths might appear to be mentally ill, and for some, this might be true. However, to the majority, they are just congested with the remnants of harmful emotional energy.

Chapter 8: How to Protect Yourself from Energy Vampires

By now you should have a fairly good understanding of what an empath is. Let's look at some new terms. When I say vampire, I'm not talking about the bloodsucking kind, although, they do suck in their own way.

First, there is a psychic vampire. This is used to describe the type of person who drains another person emotionally either empathically, meaning drying up their auric life force, or metaphorically, meaning somebody who takes emotionally but doesn't reciprocate. Psychic vampires are the type of people that were born with either an active or latent need, a physical need for life energy which they aren't able to supply themselves. They are people who have a psychological dependency on this pranic energy.

Then you have an energy vampire. This is the type of person who feeds off the energy or life force of other living creatures, mainly other people. They are sometimes also referred to as emotional vampires, energy parasites, psy-vamp, energy predator, empathic vampire, or pranic vampire.

Emotional vampirism refers to the act of manipulating another person into a desired intense emotional position like anger, passion, or love so that they can absorb the emotional energy. This vampirism includes practices like learning what a person needs in a partner and accentuating those types of traits in order to trick the person into thinking that they love them.

Now that we have covered some definitions, we can begin to look at how to stay away from these situations and be able to pick out those energy vampires.

I would like to get my PSA out of the way first. I want all empaths to know that it is okay to get rid of any relationships with a person you find out to be an energy vampire. There isn't any way to change them and it will continuously be a parasitic relationship. You will give them everything you have just to make them happy and they will just suck the life force right out of you. You will constantly feel drained, fatigued, and all around crappy. They get everything in the relationship.

Alright, back to what an energy vampire does. These people are known to make threats, manipulate people, are notorious guilt-trippers, flip out at random times, are deceptive, pick fights, cause unnecessary problems, and feed off of negative attention.

While energy vampires isn't a clinical term or diagnosis, Christiane Northrup, MD, explains that many energy vampires tend to map into "cluster B" personality disorders. These are people who tend to have erratic behavior or thinking, are overly emotional, or overly dramatic. Cluster B includes people who have narcissistic, borderline, and antisocial personality disorders. These are people whose disorders aren't caused by a chemical imbalance in the brain. Instead, they are individuals who have a somewhat misguided or a lack of a conscience or moral compass. According to Northrup, energy vampires are often those at the extreme end of this spectrum of personality disorders, mainly sociopaths and psychopaths.

For the most part, psychic vampires aren't ill-intentioned or evil. In their minds, they are victims. They think they are helpless, paranoid, powerless, strive for perfection that can never be reached, engage in extremes, self-medicate, and are preoccupied with always being right.

These people don't realize that they can create their own reality. They lack mentality. They always focus on the things that they don't have. They don't think it is possible to attain the love they desire. They don't think that they can fulfill their own needs. This means that they believe the only way to get their needs fulfilled is by taking them from others.

Empaths and highly sensitive people are more susceptible to these types of people because the emotional vampire is drawn to your warmth, bright energy, and compassion. The emotional vampire will feast on those qualities to satiate their needs until you are feeling sick and completely drained.

Empaths can be drawn to these people because they think they are in need. The thing is, energy vampires don't want to be healed. They aren't looking for somebody to save them. All they want is the attention you give them when all they have is an unnecessary and self-created problem that they crave.

These people are survivalists. As long as they are able to find a food source — you, they don't have any need to be healed or take care of themselves. The more you try to fix them, the more problems they have that start popping up.

Here are some facts. Around 20 percent of all people, female and male, have characteristics of an emotional vampire or they are full-blown vampires. That comes out to one in five people. And every one of them affects five people. That's almost 60 million people indirectly or directly affected by these people. That means that it is very likely that you are in a relationship with or know a person who is an emotional vampire.

The energy vampire could be a person you think of as a friend, a colleague, or even a parent. Chances are, though, unless you've been threatened by them, you probably don't realize that you are dealing with one because they are extremely charming, until they decided to come after you.

All of a sudden you are blindsided by insults, being shamed for all different things like how you talk, your income level, where you come from, body size, age, or social status, and you can even be abused. Energy vampires often become distant and moody, which causes you to walk on eggshells. This only causes you to expend more energy while admiring and praising them to try and keep the peace. This impacts your self-esteem so much that you believe something is really wrong with you.

When you live with this constant stress and low self-esteem caused by this person, it could lead to chronic inflammation because of your high levels of cortisol. This can cause you to indulge in other behaviors like alcohol, drugs, or bad dietary choices. This only causes more cellular inflammation and can end up leading to disease. In fact, a lot of empaths won't realize they are dealing with an energy vampire until they have become physically ill.

What really sucks is the fact that you could open your door to these people through your own insecurities. You yourself could feel powerless or feel like a victim. You could be an approval seeker. Co-dependence problems are their golden ticket.

There is a chance that you only feel good with yourself when you are helping others. You could even feel unworthy of friendships or love unless you do something. You could also feel guilty for experiencing good fortune when so many other people seem down on their luck.

You might even be addicted to energy vampires. Do you enjoy feeling needed? Do you need to please people? When you are around an energy vampire, do you feel better about yourself?

You might even be a bit of an energy vampire yourself. After you have allowed yourself to be drained by an energy vampire, do you end up draining another person? Does your only attention come from negative things?

The harsh truth is that you must be on the same vibrational level as an energy vampire to attract them. Your core beliefs and thoughts are what create these vibrations. The emotions you experience are an indication of the vibration you have.

The good news is, you can prevent this from happening. But first, let's look at how you can identify energy vampires.

Identifying Energy Vampires

As I stated above psychopaths are energy vampires, but they aren't necessarily the most common ones that you might encounter. The best way to identify vampires you are in contact with is to think of the people who came to mind while you were reading the first part of this chapter.

Not everyone that exhibits narcissistic traits or who like being the center of attention are energy vampires. There are some that recognize what they are doing, and if you say something, they will stop. However, the real energy vampires are addicted to this kind of behavior. Many energy vampires may have inherited their traits from a parent and they are completely unaware of how they affect others. The following are the six main types of energy vampires:

1. Martyr or Victim Vampire

These vampires prey off of your guilt. They believe that they are at the mercy of the world and feel they suffer mainly because of other people, instead of taking responsibility for their life. They will continually emotionally blackmail, manipulate, and blame others. Their destructive behavior is typically caused by their low self-esteem. Without constantly getting signs of approval, love, and thanks, these vampires will feel unacceptable and unworthy, which they will try to fix by making the empath feel guilty and sucking away their empathy.

2. Narcissist Vampire

This type of vampire has no capacity for empathy or any genuine interest in others. They unconsciously carry the philosophy of "Me first, you second." They constantly expect you to place them first in your life, do what they say, and feed their egos. They will manipulate you with charm but will end up stabbing you in the back. If there is a narcissist vampire in your life, you could end up feeling extremely disempowered because you are crushed under their limelight.

3. Dominator Vampire

These vampires love to feel superior and alpha. Because of their insecurities of being wrong or weak, these vampires have to overcompensate by intimidating you. They are loud-mouthed people who have strong beliefs and black and white perceptions of the world. They tend to be bigoted, sexist, or racist.

4. Melodramatic Vampire

This type of vampire thrives on creating problems. Their need for creating drama typically comes from underlying emptiness. They love to seek out crisis because it gives them the chance to feel victimized, avoidance of real issues, and an exaggerated sense of self-importance. Another reason they like creating drama is that those negative emotions are addictive.

5. Judgmental Vampire

Because these people have very low self-esteem, they love to pick on others. The way they treat people is a reflection of how they treat their own self. They love to prey on insecurities and bolstering their own egos by making others feel ashamed, pathetic, or small.

6. Innocent Vampire

All energy vampires aren't malicious, just like with innocent vampires. These can be helpless types of people who actually need help like children or friends that tend to rely on you too much. It's good when you help people you care about, but they also need to be taught how to be self-sufficient. Playing the rock in their life will erode away your energy. This means you won't have the energy for yourself.

Here are a few more traits of energy vampires, just in case you need some more clarifying facts.

1. They drain you emotionally and physically so that you can't care for yourself.

Being around these toxic people is like being anchored down in tar. It affects you on a physiological and psychological level. The entire body is affected. You may have ailments that seem to come out of thin air.

2. When you aren't around them, you could still feel their effects.

You could find yourself stewing over odd things that they said or mean things they did. You will probably feel emotionally exhausted by their craziness, their need to cause problems, or their disrespect for your basic rights and needs. Severe anxiety is often something an empath will go through when they have been around an energy vampire.

3. You feel more energetic when you are away from them for a few days or weeks.

Once you remove yourself from them, it will give you time to psychologically reset so that you are more productive, lighter, and happier. It will feel like a great weight has been removed.

4. Try to come to a simple solution with them will leave you confused and upset.

You find that you have to explain basic human integrity, fairness, and decency to them. They won't give you straight answers and they won't view you as a person.

5. They act like a needle shoved in a balloon and their actions will cause you to questions your toxicity.

Whenever you feel confident, self-assured, and joyful, they will do their best to burst your bubble with criticism and put-downs. The longer you are around them, the more you may pick up their habits.

6. There will never be any reciprocity. You are there to fulfill their needs and that's it.

They are one-sided creatures. As an empath, you will give everything and they love to take it from you. Conversations will focus on them and they are the only important person. They make decisions without considering how you might feel.

7. They down you and they take a lot of pleasure in ruining your life.

Those who are higher on the narcissistic spectrum will be pathologically envious of the people they hurt. They become jealous when they see them successful and thriving. They covet everything you have. Instead of celebrating what you achieve, they try to diminish it. They will sometimes go so far as to come up with schemes or petty ploys.

Protect Yourself

You've just learned a lot about the energy vampire and while you may know how to identify them, you may still struggle to figure out if you have been affected by them. The following will help you tell if you have been the subject of an energy vampire's attack:

- A feeling that your aura is leaking or declining is the most common symptom of a psychic attack.

- Wooziness and exhaustion are both common symptoms of an attack.

- Lack of energy.

- Muscle tension.

- Chronic headaches.

- A constant weariness and low energy levels.

- Chronic impatience, irritation, and hypertension.

- Physical ailments like the flu, cold, or other such illnesses.

As an empath, it's crucial that you know how to protect yourself against these types of people. No matter how hard you work, these types of people will still pop up in your life every now and then.

1. Commit to the things that make you happy.

Do whatever you can to increase your vibrations so high that you won't be able to be a tool for an energy vampire. Don't live your life based on what other people expect of you. Meet your own needs and set boundaries. Saying no isn't you being mean. Being a good person is not determined by how much you sacrifice.

2. Match your vibrations to the kinds of people you want to connect with.

If you want to be around people who are well adjusted, competent, and respectful, you have to project those qualities. Remove your negative core beliefs that you hold about yourself that causes vampires to come into your life. Transmute those beliefs into something positive so that others will be attracted to you.

3. Understand that Source is an infinite house of energy.

Everybody has access to their own stream of Source Energy. It is impossible to give away all of your energy or to have it taken away. Energy vampires will cause you to experience negative thoughts that can cause you to lose your connection with your Source. When this is restricted, you will start to feel depressed, confused, exhausted, and so on.

4. Make it a priority to feel good.

Get your energy flowing by doing the types of things that you love that make you energized. You must love yourself so much that you can't act like the people who exhaust you and bring you down. You deserve to have a respectful and reciprocal relationship without feeling as if you must provide and serve all of your life force.

5. Understand that they are real.

Empaths are bad to think that everybody is good and will stick to bad relationships for a lot longer than they need to by creating excuses for the other person. Understanding that there are those out there who aren't good is going to help you protect yourself.

6. Follow your gut.

Empaths are extremely intuitive. After you have been around a vampire, this ability will sometimes wan. One way to gain back your gut is to journal. Make sure that you pay attention to the things your body says about others.

7. Say no.

This is the number one way to protect yourself. This will minimize the interactions you have with these people. You must know how to turn people down. This is going to take some practice. If you aren't able to say no, try to say something like "I'll get back to you." The most important thing is to stop saying yes automatically.

8. Find some support.

It's important that you find support once you fully understand your gift. This isn't just a good friend. This means finding a therapist who specializes in this type of problem. There are even some recovery groups.

9. Cut them out of your life if you can.

If you aren't constantly around them, then remove all contact. If you aren't able to, then try to cut out as much communication as you possibly can. If it is an ex-spouse with whom you share children, only text them when you communicate instead of talking in person.

10. Come up with strong boundaries.

Figure out the activities that you are able to handle with them. You might be able to handle them when you are in public places, but you don't want to be left alone with them in your house. It also helps to set beginning and end times.

11. Be the wet blanket.

Don't do things that will entertain them. This will make sure that they can't access your energy. Don't give them the response that they want and they will lose interest.

12. Differentiate between dumping and venting.

Everybody needs to voice their frustrations every now and then. Energy vampires love to dump their negative feelings, annoyances, irritations, bad days, and frustrations to everybody around them. People who vent know what role they played in their problem and want to find a solution. Dumping is mainly an unintelligible rant.

13. Keep yourself from overreacting.

Do whatever it takes for you to remain cool, calm, and collected around these types of people. Losing your cool is only going to give them what they were looking to get.

Chapter 9: Problems that Empathy can Cause

Because of all the energy that empaths take in, there is going to be some negative side effects. These can manifest into actual physical ailments. Empaths could experience a sudden onset of chronic fatigue because of a large crash in their energy level.

This is caused by a variety of emotional responsibilities since empaths leak their own energy when they can't stay in the present, balanced, grounded, and consciously aware.

Empaths often feel drained when they have been around people because these interactions can create emotional exhaustion. Empaths need a lot of alone time to be able to recharge their emotional batteries and retreat from society.

Our thoughts, feelings, and emotions can wreak havoc on the internal systems of an empath. This can cause devastating consequences that can leave them feeling debilitated. When empaths don't have space where they can quiet their minds, they can become overactive at night. This prevents them from being able to relax and get to sleep.

Their hyperactive mind will cause them to feel fatigued by the constant bombardment of stimuli. This doesn't let them replenish, recharge, and rest. This causes them to have erratic sleep patterns. Some days they might require ten or more hours of sleep, where other nights they might only need one or two.

Emotional feelings that are linked to memories could cause an empath to feel emotions like panic, paranoia, resentment, anxiety, and fear, so their brains become convinced they are under an actual threat. Therefore, the brain will signal the adrenal glands to produce hormones and this releases a surge of energy.

When empaths are exposed to intense of prolonged stress or anxiety, or they have an unhealthy lifestyle like a general life crisis, stressful family situations, stressful relationships, poor diet, substance abuse, overworking, or too little or too much sleep, they put a lot of demand on their adrenal glands.

These endocrine glands are the size of a walnut and shaped like a kidney. They are located just above the kidneys. They are great when you are under stress, but when they get over-stimulated, they will continue to produce energy which can leave the empath permanently wired and on high alert. In the end, they become burned out and malfunction.

When the adrenal gland is working properly, you might feel continuously fatigued, overwhelmed, anxious, rundown, dizzy, and irritable. You might experience high or low blood sugar, sugar or salt cravings, heart palpitations, and you might find it hard to deal with stressful situations.

During sleep, cortisol levels, which are produced by the adrenal glands, will naturally rise and peak a few hours before you get up. This is meant to give us a good start to our day. This is known as the circadian rhythm.

If you have exhausted adrenal glands, you might wake up feeling tired, even if you slept through the entire night. You might even feel drowsy during the majority of the day, but then cortisol peaks during the late evening and it makes it hard for you to go to sleep.

It will take some time for your adrenal glands to wear down, so it takes just as long to fully repair them. There are changes, though, that can have an immediate effect. The most important thing to do is make sure you listen to your body and pay close attention to the way you feel.

In order to keep your adrenal glands nourished and to avoid adrenal fatigue, you can eat a nutritional, organic, and well-balanced diet that has lots of protein and plenty of vitamins A, B, and C. Be sure that you are giving your body plenty of time to absorb these nutrients before you do any type of physical activity. It is also important that you stay away from drinking a lot of alcohol and reduce or get rid of refined salt, caffeine, and refined sugar intake.

By creating some security, getting lots of sleep, being optimistic, finding inner peace, stability, and joy will help you rebalance your adrenal glands. Just the thought of going to bed could cause some anxiety if we think we are going to be awake for hours, drifting in and out of sleep, but never reaching that much-needed delta state.

Meditation can help empaths to focus on their body so that they are aware of all sensations that are happening and it could help them soothe and calm their mind so they don't continue to repeat negative thought through their brain that is going to cause a chemical reaction.

Spending time with family and friends or going to social outing could also help re-regulate their cortisol levels. This is because they are known to increase when they spend a long time by themselves. This means that they will feel separated, lonely, and isolated. If an empath feels content in their own company, they will feel balanced and their cortisol levels won't become an issue.

Their exercise and diet program could also add stress to their adrenal glands. If they push their bodies too much, there might be too much demand on their adrenal glands. This could cause them to produce too much of the stress-related hormones.

Intense workout, skipping meals, and eating junk foods could cause the adrenal glands to become overworked. If an empath has food allergies, this could put even more stress on their glands, so it is important for them to pay attention to the food intolerances they have.

If the adrenal glands get fatigued, you might wake up during the night on high alert from a dream that was very stimulating. This will just add to your overanxious state.

Sleepless nights are more common when you endure anxious and stressful periods because even if you can go to sleep, you might wake up during the night feeling the adrenaline coursing through your veins but not knowing why. These sleep disturbances are closely linked to biochemical reactions because of high levels of stress hormones through the body at around two to four AM. This spike in your hormones will dramatically affect your ability to stay calm, which is the reason why your sleep gets interrupted.

This could be fixed through making up some magical and therapeutic potions with unrefined salt and organic honey. It is also helpful to have a Himalayan salt lamp by your bed. This will get rid of positive ions in the environment and replace them with negative ions, which mimics the balance in nature. It will also help to get rid of electric smog that your electronic devices cause so that the air remains clear. This means you will have improved air circulation and be able to breathe better.

Chapter 10: How to Handle Empathy in Your Life

Everyone would love to find their soul mate, have close friends and connect to their family. However, empathic people often struggle in this area for many reasons. Romance is very hard for an empath.

An empathic person has a tendency to have a hard time when finding romance. It is interesting when you know two empaths who each have mental scars get together. They have a very hard time getting past feeling the other's hidden issues and pains.

They might spend hours arguing with the other about how they know something is wrong just to have the other say they knew their partner was upset.

The real problems are in these things:

1. Empaths can scare the crap out of you.

It could be exciting, especially if you are an empath to meet another empath that could potentially be your romantic partner. You would think they could express their feelings better than people who aren't empaths. They do because they know their feelings, unlike normal people who like to second guess their feelings. This means, it might be weeks into your relationships and they might tell you "I love you." Nothing will be able to change an empaths mind about how they feel. This could ruin the relationship at times.

2. Inconsistency could create more struggles.

Empaths don't like it when what people say don't match what they do or what they feel because empaths can pick up on all this stuff. It is tough on them when they have to call out their family, friends, and partners. This can become very rough if they are living in close quarters with loved ones. Empaths can pick up on every little smudge on the surface of honesty.

3. Empaths can be moody.

This is hard for relationships and friendships. Due to their strong emotions, things can get out of control at times. Most of the time, the feelings that go through an empath's body won't be their own. The main problem is they might have absorbed too much energy from their loved one. This might wind up being sent back to the original owner of that particular emotion. It is very unfair that the empath will get blamed for this, but this is how it usually works out.

4. Empaths can pick up on complacency.

You know how some relationships eventually reach a plateau? Empaths can sense this before it happens. Every new relationship is going to reach a point where things taper off and settle. This isn't a bad thing. It just means the relationship has leveled out.

An empath will notice and might begin to panic. They might begin stirring up trouble just to get some intensity back into the relationship. If their partner can't sense this, they might think the empath is being very strange. In reality, it is nothing but a gift that has gone awry.

5. Empaths need their own space but don't like to be alone, either.

This is such a lovely conundrum, isn't it? It might seem strange, but if you analyze it the right way, it does make sense. Empaths love being in love and they love to spend time with their partner. They also need to have a space of their own when they need it. They will be more emotional when they don't have their personal time. They need to have time to recuperate and energize themselves.

6. Empaths won't give up.

Empaths will not break up, divorce, or dissolve a romantic relationship or any relationship for that matter. It doesn't matter if this is their best option. Empathic people will always see the potential in other people because they can feel the frustration in the relationship. This struggle happens when an empath is married to someone who is not in touch with their feelings and the word divorce comes up in conversation. The empath will want to hold things together no matter what. Imagine that there is a person more compatible for the empath but they won't know it because they are going to continue to try to revive what they have already lost.

7. They never get taken seriously.

This is the largest problem for any relationship an empath has whether it is romantic or not. They are going to have ideas that are going to sound far-fetched but if they can be given the benefit of the doubt, they will convince people just how much their words mean. This is usually a struggle for many relationships because most people just say things and will only do them about 40 percent of the time.

People are used to just believing less than half of what others say, especially in a close relationship. The thing is, empaths will tell you they can do something and can actually do it. This is why it hurts so much when other people don't believe them.

It is important that the empaths' friends, family, and romantic partners take them seriously. Empaths are the most real people out there and that is why they usually struggle in their relationships.

Relationship Sabotage

As you might have figured out by now, empaths are prone to having more relationship problems than normal people do. They also respond to these problems differently and in unusual ways. These ways are not always healthy. Here is a list of different ways an empath might sabotage their relationship.

- They won't stop expressing their own needs.

Empaths get so focused on making their partner happy that they end up neglecting their own self. An empath is very prone to forget how important it is for them to express their needs and making sure they get met. This can cause things to happen that will harm the relationship. The empath begins to feel neglected and their partner isn't going to understand.

- They compromise boundaries without being asked to.

Empaths will often feel their partner's needs in such a profound way that they decide to give into them in ways that will end up hurting them. They might choose to negate a boundary that their partner didn't ask them to cross. When they make this decision without letting their partner know, the empath is opening themselves up to anger and resentment. Their partner won't understand what happened. They will become confused and frustrated because of it.

- They don't take care of themselves.

Because empaths are so concerned with other people's emotional well-being, they will often neglect themselves. When they get too focused on another person, they will sometimes neglect the things that make them who they are. This might mean that they spend less time with their friends, less energy for things they like to do, and less focus on their work that they find meaningful. This can cause their self-esteem and happiness to suffer.

- Important problems get solved in their head.

It is common for an empath to keep a running dialogue in their head and they will take on both sides of the argument. The empath will often resolve the issue in their head and they won't even bring up the issue. This might get rid of the problem, but it could just as easily create new ones. It is very unfair to their partner who isn't even aware that there is a conflict. It robs them of autonomy, their chance to defend their self, and the opportunity to understand the empaths viewpoint.

Be sure that if you are an empath you don't become prey to your own devices. Try to find these behaviors and fight them so you can create a healthy relationship.

Empathy at Work

Studies have been done and found out that people who work together can "catch" another's emotions. This means that one person's panic could spread through the office like flu. This will lower productivity and morale. The opposite could also be true and happiness might build in the workplace. This will result in improved performance, satisfaction, and cooperation.

The problem for empaths is that these feelings are stronger. These feeling are amplified in them. The good thing is, though, empaths are also able to benefit from positivity that runs through the office. The hard thing happens when they pick up on illnesses and negative emotions.

Everyone is going to have bad days. Unfortunately for empaths, a bad day for one co-worker might mean a bad day for them, too. Many offices now are "open concept." This means that desks don't have walls separating them or they are made up of cubicles with glass partitions. This means that everyone uses the same space. People are able to hear all the candy wrappers being opened, someone snapping their gum, laughing, humming, blowing noses, gossiping, talking, complaining, and coughing. You are able to smell everyone's perfume, what they ate for lunch, and you can see everyone moving around. This puts you on sensory overload. Having very little privacy makes an empath vulnerable to their co-worker's stress.

But there are some pretty effective solutions. Shopify asked their employees about this and discovered that there was a balance between extroverts and introverts. They had office designers modify the workplace to accommodate each group. Some of the sections were more interactive and noisier.

Then there were other offices that with couches that had high backs that they could move into the corner to create some privacy and they made designated rooms that looked like libraries for quiet work. This new design element offered the introverts more peacefulness and space to work. Because of this design, they weren't as exposed to the stress of their office-mates.

Empaths also have to deal with the emotions of their clients, even when they are just talking on the phone. To deal with this problem, the following are some ways to create boundaries for your energy at work.

- If you work in a chaotic office, fill the edges of your workspace with happy photos and plants to make a psychological barrier. You could also use sacred objects or healings stones to create a boundary for your energy.

- Take breaks or take a few minutes outside to get a reprieve from the noise.

- If you are allowed to, use noise-canceling headphones so you can muffle out some of the noise from your surrounding areas.

- It might help to visualize a golden light enveloping your complete workstation that will repel any negativity and lets positive energy in.

Any of these techniques are going to help you create a wall of protection so you don't fall prey to the emotions of the people you work with.

Chapter 11: Become More Self-Aware

In order to understand other people, we have to understand ourselves. We need to teach people that we are all made up of different personalities like our inner critic or our happy voice. Our goal is to recognize all the parts of our personalities to become more aware of our patterns and tendencies. This helps us navigate relationships and the way we connect with others.

When we can improve the different parts of our personalities, we also improve the ability to understand other people's mental states. This is called empathy or theory of mind.

Empathy and self-awareness are intimately connected. When we get more aware of what makes us the person we are, we can understand the difference between others and ourselves and what makes them the person they are.

It isn't surprising to know that empathy and self-awareness are the two main characteristics behind emotional intelligence. Empathy is being aware of others and its counterpart is self-awareness.

Once you become aware of yourself, you will become aware of others. The self will be clearer and you will start to see the ways you are different and similar to others in the way you feel and think.

This is an important part of empathy, it isn't about finding ways you are like others but seeing the ways you are different. You can easily empathize with other people when you think they are just like you. It isn't trying to understand their perspective, it is just projecting your perspective onto them.

You might be an introvert but you understand that everybody isn't going to be just like you. When you meet a person who is more extroverted, it shouldn't surprise or frustrate you. Just realize that you both have different tendencies and personalities and keep this in mind when you are around them.

There are ways you can start to improve your self-awareness that you can begin right now:

- Meditation

This is the best way to improve self-awareness. If you are a beginner, just learning how to breathe will help you tremendously. Doing breathing meditation is a wonderful way to become aware of your feelings and thoughts as you begin to accept them without judgment. Meditation can teach you how you can look at your surroundings and yourself without having to react. It is a wonderful way to self-regulate. This is another aspect of emotional intelligence.

- Personality Quizzes

If you can learn more about your personality, it will help you understand how your mind works and how it is different from other people. There are free surveys that will help you get a better understanding of the real you. These will show you different traits such as introversion, extraversion, big picture, and detail oriented. Your score on these quizzes will bring some insight into the type of personality you have.

- Contemplation

Meditation helps you watch your feelings and thoughts. Contemplation helps you analyze your mind and learn about your thought process. Taking 10 to 15 minutes every day to sit down and analyze your thoughts and beliefs is a great way to be aware of the way your mind works.

- Role-playing

One way to figure out more about you is to pretend to be someone else. When you practice this, it might reveal some hidden aspects of yourself that you aren't aware of. When you try to be someone who is very different than you, it will show you what will or won't fit into your personality.

- Ask Friends

Many times our family and friends know more about us than we do. Some personality traits get so deeply ingrained that we just take them for granted. A good way to increase your self-awareness is to ask a friend. Ask them to describe you as a person. This might reveal some patterns that they see in us that we can't see for ourselves. Friends are good at seeing our extroversion, creativity, and intelligence.

These are great ways to begin improving our self-awareness. Will we ever be able to completely know ourselves? That is one question that doesn't have an answer. We are complicated beings and it might be possible to never totally grasp who we really are.

If we can actively build self-awareness, it will help you improve yourself and your ability to connect with others in a meaningful and genuine way.

Remember how important self-awareness is and try some of the exercises above to start improving it.

Chapter 12: Normalizing, Fine Tuning and Maintaining Your Gift

Understanding your gift is one thing, embracing it and helping it grow is another. It's important that you feel comfortable and normal with your gift because it makes you who you are. The exercises in this chapter will help you to fine-tune your abilities so that you can be the best empath possible.

- Challenge yourself – Undertake some challenging experiences which will push you past your comfort zone. Try learning something new like a foreign language, hobby, or instrument. Create a new competency. Doing this is going to humble you and humility is important for enabling empathy.

- Move outside of your normal environment – Travel, especially to a place with new cultures. This will help you to appreciate others.

- Receive feedback – Ask your colleagues, family, and friends for feedback about your relationship skills and then check in with them every now and then.

- Get to know your heart and not just your head – Read books that explore personal emotions and relationships. This has been proven to help improve the empathy of new doctors.

- Take a moment to walk in somebody else's shoes – Talk with other people about what it is like to be them. Ask about their concerns and issues and how they view experiences that you both have experienced.

- Look at your biases – Everybody has hidden and not-so-hidden biases that can interfere with their ability to empathize. These tend to be centered on visible factors like gender, age, and race. Don't believe you have any sort of biases? Think again, everybody does.

- Create some curiosity – What are you able to learn from some colleagues who are "inexperienced?" What might will you be able to learn from a client you have claimed is "narrow?" People who are curious will ask a lot of questions which leads them to create a stronger understanding of those around them.

- Ask questions – Make sure that you have some questions to ask when you are having a conversation.

- Take a class – There are online courses for empaths that can help you to practice your skills and nurture your abilities.

- Talk with an expert – Find a person who you think has strong empathy skills. Ask them how they have improved their abilities.

- Expand your imagination – When you are working to see things from another's point of view, try putting together everything that you know about them and create an inner picture. Based on the picture you have created, try to see what the world looks like through their eyes.

- Learn the art of listening – The more actively you listen which means you hear what they say without judging or preparing what you are going to say, the more you will learn about their side. In order to listen actively, you have to turn off your "internal judge" when a person is talking.

Controlling Emotions

Overactive empathy happens when you open up to the emotions of others, but you aren't able to return to normal. This means you are left out there to absorb other people's stuff. When you are in social gatherings, you are able to sense everything that other's feel and think.

This can lead to self-neglect, people pleasing, and self-sacrifice. This is something that many empaths will struggle with. If you find yourself experiencing overactive empathy, it's important that you control the emotions and become more centered. To control your emotions, all you need are these tips:

1. Notice your feelings

Tune back into what are your real feelings. You have to check, at the very least once a day with yourself to see how you feel. Keep a log that you fill in before bed that explains the emotions you went through that day. When somebody asks you for a favor, before saying yes, check with yourself to see how you feel. Don't respond to only their needs. Center yourself so that you know how you feel about the task.

2. Talk to your source to remove energies you don't need

If you start to feel emotionally overwhelmed or you feel like you have lost yourself, take three deep breaths and say this prayer:

"I call upon Source/God to clear my energy field of all energies that are not serving me. So it is."

You can even come up with your own prayer if you want. There's no need for it to be long or complicated. This is a very powerful clearing technique.

3. Allow yourself to enjoy you

The majority of empaths rarely have fun when they have to interact with others. They go into situations with the belief that they have to help those who are not happy or well. They feel responsible and dutiful for the people's feelings.

To fix this, focus on trying to have fun in how you interact. If you find that you aren't into a conversation with somebody, then don't engage with them. If the person you are talking to is draining you, pull back. Your enjoyment should be put first when in a social gathering. Don't focus so much on. This might sound selfish, but empaths have to establish boundaries to control their emotions.

Chapter 13: Keeping Out Unwanted Emotions

While being an empath is a great skill, what do you do if you start getting overwhelmed by other's negative emotions? The good news is that there are ways to stop absorbing the feelings of other people while still being a good empath.

Being empathic is normal for many humans, especially empaths. Empathy can be found in all animals that are social like mice and primates. The majority of people evolve their empathy from parental instincts. All parents, animal or human, will tune into their children so that they bond with them and can figure out when they are in distress. This is the reason why a lot of adults don't like to hear a baby cry or we start laughing when a baby giggles. Empathy is why we sneeze or yawn when somebody else does it. We also tend to mimic the facial expressions and body language of others. The brain is made that way.

Not only can an empath catch a person's yawn, they actually catch their moods. This can be great when your friend is happy and they give you a mood boost. But it gets exhausting when your boss's anxiety, partner's stress, co-worker's grief, or the crankiness of the teenager at the McDonalds infects you. Secondhand stress or anger is like secondhand smoke.

With growing research, it's easy to notice how negativity caught from each other can impact a person's educational and business outcome. It can also impact the empath on a cellular level and if not handled, it can shorten their lifespan. There are some hotels that have noticed the problem with secondhand stress and have started to create "no venting" zones where the employees aren't allowed to vent around customers. If an empath goes to the doctor and feels the nurse seething with anger, they are likely to catch the anger and it could end up affecting the doctor's visit.

What can we do about this without isolating our self from society altogether and live as a hermit? This is going to take boundaries and a change in your perspective to make sure you stay protected from the emotions of others.

1. Label their feelings

When you are able to label another person's emotions, it will create some distance between you and the emotion. It will give you some time to reflect so that you can deal with it and figure out how to react. It will help you to deal with emotions that are negative. It will help you if you have to respond to your child's meltdown. By saying "so and so" is feeling "this way," you state that they are feeling that way and you aren't. Language will create a barrier between your thoughts and feelings and will lessen the strength of the emotions.

2. Limit social media and negativity

We no longer only deal with information overload, we have to face emotional overload. This can be stressful for the empath. You click into Facebook and you are bombarded with your friend's emotions of hungry, mad, sad, and any other emotion you can think of. Twitter is another home for extreme emotions. When some form of tragedy strikes and the story hits the news, everybody' emotions will get added to yours. You are now more connected to people than ever before whether you realize it or not. Those people on social media will influence you daily.

You have to learn how to be selective with your exposure to news media and social media. Remove friends who always post horrible passive-aggressive things that are aimed at people they hate. If you need a break from the real news, try reading The Onion for some satirical things. Never, EVER, read comments. They are the quickest way to get sucked down an emotional rabbit hole.

3. Create limits

If you surround yourself with chronic complainers or negative people, you will have to learn how to deflect their negativity. You must eliminate or reduce the time you spend around them. This is going to be hard if you work in a toxic environment. If your family tends to constantly stress, even though they are family, you must limit the amount of time you spend around them. You may discover that you have to break off friendships that you've had since grade school. You can't help anybody if your emotions are constantly being sabotaged. It may be hard to realize this, but after you move away and leave all of this negativity behind, your life is going to get calmer.

4. Create a wall of positivity

There is no way to block out all negative emotions, but you can also increase positive ones. It always sounds corny when you are told to practice positivity and gratitude, but if you are able to make it a part of your everyday life, your happiness is going to increase. Try some gratitude when you end up crying over somebody else's hurt. This can also work if you see something on television that is upsetting. This will help you to remember and feel all of the good times in your life and in the world even though you are experiencing negativity.

If you are able to build up a wall of immunity, it is going to help you take care of your wellbeing and self-esteem. The best buffer you can have against other's stress is to have a strong and stable self-esteem. If your self-esteem is high, you are going to be able to handle situations more easily. When you notice that you are being hindered by the moods of others, take a moment and to remind yourself that things are great and that you can handle it. Exercise is another great way to improve your self-esteem because the brain will make a record of the times that you exercise by releasing endorphins.

Before you face a stressful moment, give yourself a shot of gratitude. Before you start your day, the first thing you should do is think of three things that you are grateful of. Here are five other things that you can do each day to boost your brain against negativity:

- Two-minute meditation
- 30 minutes of cardio

- Two minutes writing down positive experiences
- Write down a few things you are grateful for
- Send a friend an email praising them for what they accomplished

Make sure you spend a lot of time that is positive and joyful. This doesn't mean everybody must be uplifting 24 hours a day seven days a week. Just being around a person who tends to generally be happy is going to give you a boost for your positivity wall. Your favorite song or the sound of a child's laughter can boost your mood if you are having a really bad day.

5. Change to compassion

Learning how to change your empathy into compassion is a great technique. Compassion is very different than empathy. Different parts of the brain are triggered when you share another person's pain or if you respond to their suffering.

Figuring out the difference between the two is important. As an empath, you are constantly feeling another person's pain and suffering. These moments can be so intense that it creates real distress inside of you. But if you can learn to feel compassion for the person, you won't take in as much of their energy. You will feel concerned for them and you will feel more motivated to help them.

Using techniques such as meditation will enforce a loving kindness that will help your brain to shift your empathy into compassion. Basically, you have to learn the art of detached attachment.

6. Create lighter discussion

There are some negative attitudes that get triggered by seemingly harmless topics. Your friend could turn into a toxic self-victimizer when you start talking about their job. No matter what is said, they constantly complain about everything and when you try to add in some positive things, they ignore them completely and spews out more negativity. This will become a conversation dampener.

When you find yourself in a moment like this and the person you are conversing with is stuck on something that is bringing you down, realize that those negative feelings are probably deeply rooted. The best thing that you could do is to bring up a new topic that can lighten the mood. Bring up things like funny memories, friendships, success stories, and other types of happy news that can create a lighter conversation. Stick to things that they feel positive about.

7. Release the want to change a person's negative tendencies

Some people can be helped by creating a good example for them, others you can't. When you can recognize the difference, it'll help maintain your equilibrium. Don't let energy vampires, emotional blackmailers, and manipulators control you by trying to control something you can't, which are other people's behaviors.

That said, if there is a behavior that somebody you love has that you hope will change, it likely won't. If you are in desperate need for them to change, be honest with them and lay all your cards out so that they know how and why you feel that way.

For the most part, you won't be able to change people and you need to quit trying. You either have to accept who they are or you have to live without them. This may sound harsh, but really it isn't. When you try to change a person, they will resist and stay exactly the same, but when you don't try to change them and you support them, they may gradually change. What changes the most is the way that you view them.

Chapter 14: Healing

You've likely started to wonder if being an empath is a blessing or a curse. Ask any empath, they may say it's a curse. The extreme empaths could tell you it's a death sentence. If some are able to see it as a gift, why do so many hate it? Do empaths really have a purpose?

Most intuitive is an empath to a certain degree. If they weren't, then they wouldn't be able to tap into the energy of other people or feel their spirit. Let's talk about those who don't only feel anxieties, emotions, and illnesses of others but they manifest the feelings as their own.

If you have run across a person who is always in some form of pain, feels tired all the time, and has some unexplained illnesses, these are likely empaths. These people aren't hypochondriacs. They haven't been able to figure out how to deal with their abilities. Empaths will often get sick and tired faster than the average person. This is because they consume a lot of bad energies and don't realize it. They allow the energy to build in them until it becomes a physical condition. It could be lethargy, illness, or anxiety.

If you notice that you are experiencing anxiety or depression, it could be other people's energies and emotions. It's important that you figure out a way of getting rid of the old energy, reset yourself, and learn the best way to protect yourself from the energy of others. Working with a coach could be helpful since they can help you learn specific techniques and lessons that you can continue to use throughout your life.

While there may be times where being an empath feels like a curse, but it is honestly a gift. Once you have figured out the best way to use your gift, you find that you can help a lot of other people.

Empaths make perfect healers. They are able to sense the pain in others and can help them to heal it. Most people don't even realize where their emotional pain is resonating from, empaths can help. They have the ability to sense out the bad energy so why not use it? Empaths are also great reiki practitioners, truth-seers, and spiritual coaches.

Are you an empath, but you're not interested in working in the spiritual world? That's fine. They are also perfect as nurses, firemen, hospice caregivers, and acupuncturists. These are all healing fields that are great for the empath.

Empaths are the perfect healers because they are able to feel things on such a deep level. It probably sounds crazy to be an empath and work in areas that put you close to other's energy, but that's what you were born to do.

You will find that you take in others energy, but there are plenty of ways to release it without allowing it to boil under the surface, which will turn into anxiety or illness. It's important that you manage your gift and in doing so, you will improve your life. Once you have figured out how to identify your emotions and energy and you know how to release it, everything will become easier and you will be able to align with your purpose. You will become the healer you were meant to be.

A lot of empaths will try to hide away from the world. This may sound good in theory, but it's not teaching them how to handle energy. With time empaths can learn a lot of healing techniques so that they can live a completely full life.

There is going to be a shift when you focus on being all that you can be instead of just trying to survive. This is when you will allow yourself to awaken fully. You will shift from feeling as if it's a curse and embrace it. Let's take a look at how you can learn how to release past experiences and clean out what isn't serving you so that you can heal. Anybody can use these techniques, empath or not, to create a life change. The point is to realize that you have to start where you are. You aren't trying to create a new version of yourself. This will be a disservice to any real work that you try. You have to be transparent with yourself and this will take a lot of courage, but it is the most important step.

You can and should put your needs first. This may sound like it goes against what an empath is, but this has to be done from the very start. It's important to understand that everything in the Universe is energy and that everything is connected. Many of these techniques are going to work with the spiritual realm and energy. As long as you keep your mind open, everything will work. There are a lot of steps along your path to healing. It will take some time before you can settle into a rhythm that will feel right and safe. Everybody can heal misalignments and diseases that are inside us with intention, open minds, imagination, and a warm heart. Everything is just a part of the ritual that you will use to put yourself in a state of being so that your inner healer is able to help others. You will need to trust the unknown for these practices to work. They will take some magic, creativity, imagination, and faith.

Most empaths, unfortunately, have suffered at the hands of somebody that they loved deeply. From years of unmet childhood needs, not being understood, a lot of empaths suffer from distrust and low self-esteem. They've suffered rejection or ridicules because they are sensitive and they could be defensive about it or they suppress their self completely. A lot of them will have trust issues that are so bad they can't even trust their self. They likely feel as if their own bodies and emotions betray them. People close to them may have abandoned them during moments of need. This will often create a pattern in their relationships where they try to find others who match that part. With practice, they will be able to figure out the reason behind abandoning their self when their emotions become too much.

The biggest shift is going to come when you realize that there is no need for you to sacrifice your happiness for somebody else. Once you understand that your feelings matter, that your emotions and thoughts matter, you will be able to come up with a way to handle overwhelming negative emotions. You could find yourself at a point in your life where it feels like caring for somebody means you must give them your last breath. You will likely neglect your needs to show those around you that you care. There is likely going to be times when people mistake your kindness for weakness.

In order for you to nurture your wholeness and happiness, you will need to learn how to express to others the things that don't serve your wellbeing.

You must stop doing the following:

- People pleasing
- Enabling behavior that is destructive
- Doing other's work
- Being a scapegoat for another's unresolved trauma
- Spending time with others because you feel guilty
- Providing a person energy who doesn't care about your time or feelings
- Allowing yourself to be a victim
- Being codependent

Empaths will face a lot of damage from narcissists. Since there is a constant barrage of emotions coming at the empath, there will likely be wounds created that can't heal. It may often seem impossible to deal with your issues while carrying other's baggage. We are going to look at a few ways to heal from your past and heal for the future.

As I mentioned earlier, most empaths were probably ridiculed or made fun of as a child. People didn't understand them, so they made fun. What some may see as small jokes carve a deep scar into an empath. All they want is to be accepted by people they care about, so when those they love criticize them for who they are, it hurts.

Oftentimes, an empath may not have faced being made fun of for their sensitivity, instead, they had a traumatic childhood in general. During childhood, they may have been surrounded by criminal behavior, mental illness, substance abuse, or violence. This then led to empathy.

Either way, scars have been made and those have to be healed. Luckily, there are several ways you can heal your childhood now to help you with your empathy.

1. Reframe

You can't change what happened, unfortunately, but you can control the way you experience it now. Instead of allowing yourself to respond in the same way you did when a disturbing incident pops in your mind, take a moment to pause and breathe. Then take a moment to reinterpret that memory. Ask, "How did this make me stronger?"

2. Get rid of shame

Unlike guilt or remorse, shame has nothing to do about feeling bad for what you did, instead, it's feeling bad for what you are. Shame kills your spirit. This is where feelings of undeserving, worthlessness, and unlovable come from. Oftentimes, childhood troubles will cause shame which you try to treat by making "psychic promises." These are things like say "I'll act like my parents so that they will treat me better." "If I get rid of my feelings, I won't have to experience the pain."

To keep these contracts from destroying you, figure out what promises you made and allow yourself to break them. Shame is a lie, don't listen to it. You are worthy of respect and love.

3. Let go of the pain

Research has found that people who write down their past traumas will heal faster. Take some time to write out letters to those who hurt you. Nobody ever has to see them, so you don't have to censor yourself. Let out all of your rages on that piece of paper. To take it a step further, burn the paper once you have written the letter. This will act like an even bigger release.

4. Stop regret

Having the repetition of "I should have…" and "If only…" statements will destroy your health and your peace of mind. To heal, you have to stop punishing yourself for previous mistakes. Forgive yourself, learn the lessons you need to, and resolve to perform differently in the future. Take a look back at regrettable things and recall who you were then. What did and didn't you know at that time? What choices did you have? By reviewing the scenario, you could discover that you did the best you could at that time.

5. From grief to gain

Emotional wounds are as real as physical wounds. To mend them, you will have to move through three phases of grief: shock/denial, anger/sadness/fear, and understanding/acceptance. Many people get stuck in the shock/denial phase. You can move past that stage and find yourself bogged down in chronic anger or fear. Either way, your healing isn't complete. No matter how long ago it was, you have to allow yourself to feel the emotions that you suppressed. Find ways to express those emotions so that you can move to phase three, understanding and acceptance.

6. Create gratitude

Gratitude is better than acceptance. No matter the things that happened to you, tell yourself that you have gifts that you should be thankful for. You could even find that you are grateful for your troubles because they have shaped you today.

7. Satisfying future

Living well is the best revenge. The best way to find peace with your past is to be the person you are meant to be. The grip of old perceptions and patterns can be strong to the point that you feel like a helpless victim. In fact, you are the creator of your life and a new scene can be started at any time.

8. Acceptance

This acceptance doesn't have to do with your past. Instead, once you have worked through your past, you must accept the fact that you are an empath. Quit wondering if you might be. Accept yourself for who you are. Empaths are beautiful people.

9. Own it

Once you have accepted the fact that you are an empath, allow it to be a part of you. Be proud and own your existence. It's believed that around one in 20 people is a true empath, so take pride in your sensitivities. This is the only way to make sure you quit feeling like you're a victim.

10. Meditate

Meditation is such an important thing for an empath. There are hundreds of different techniques that you can try. Find what works for you. Some people will use music or white noise. Others have to have complete silence. Explore different things and use what you like.

11. Love it

Now that you accept and own the fact that you're an empath, you now need to love it. You are special and unique. You are a blessing in other's lives. Other people are not a burden. Being an empath is only a single part of you. This isn't a condition that has to be treated.

12. Create boundaries

Boundaries are extremely crucial. View these boundaries as lines in the sand. Those in your life need to stay on their side. If they cross the line, you will be able to distance yourself. Be honest about these boundaries. They shouldn't be invisible. The hardest thing for an empath is getting rid of those people who don't respect their boundaries.

Important Truths

A person's energy will tell you more about them than their words will. As a child, you were likely quiet and shy. You wanted to watch people instead of getting involved. You probably picked up on nuances and undercurrents of thoughts and emotions.

Pain, people, energy, faces, sensations, words, feelings, and meaning — you are likely about to feel all of these. It could make you feel sick. When you learn that you're an empath, you will find a new door to healing and self-discovery. You will no longer be alone.

The following are eight important truths that you are going to discover as an empath:

1. You don't have to take on a person's pain.

As an empath, you can feel other's pain and you will internalize it. What you need to remember is that you can only do so much. You can guide others to help them as much as you can, but they have to help themselves in order to heal. An empath's nature will blind them to this fact. There are a lot of people who don't want to be fixed because they are comfortable in their misery.

2. Accept the pain, don't escape it.

This will allow you to release the energy in you. When you focus on trying to escape or repress pain, you will cause a cycle of suffering. Quit running and sit down and let yourself experience fatigue, hurt, confusion, and anger. This will allow you to let it go.

3. You could project your emotions on others.

As an empath, you have a bit of an escape hatch. It creates an opportunity to blame others. You soak up emotions like a sponge, but that doesn't mean you don't create experiences of your own. It is very easy for empaths to act the victim. It's harder to accept your happiness. You have to distinguish your feelings from other's feelings and sometimes there may not be a clear distinction.

4. Self-esteem is important for an empath.

Empaths with low self-esteem will suffer more than those who have a healthy self-esteem. This isn't always obvious. It's quite easy to blame feelings of hopelessness and worthlessness on the energy that you have absorbed. Once you realize you can create trust, respect, and love inside yourself, your suffering will stop.

5. Being an empath is different than having empathy.

Empathy and compassion are not the same. It doesn't mean you feel sorry for others and you want to help them out. Empathy is looking past what people say or do and understanding their values, feelings, beliefs, and situations. Having empathy is being able to understand people and walking in their shoes. Empathy is intellectual and emotional. Being an empath is an emotional, physical, and kinesthetic experience. You can share a person's feelings, but you might not understand it on a deeper level. Understanding the difference between empath and empathy will help you grow so that you can create empathy.

6. Shielding doesn't always help.

Shielding can help temporarily, but it won't help for long. Shielding means you are resisting the energy of other's and this only causes more pain and fear for you. Open yourself up to emotions instead of fighting them. Allow yourself to experience this and let them go. This will take practice.

7. Mindfulness and catharsis are great.

Incorporating catharsis into your life is important for releasing bad energy. Helpful forms of catharsis include journaling, jogging, writing, walking, and meditation. Singing, crying, laughing, dancing, and privately screaming can also help. You also need to learn how to tune into your body. This can help you to anchor yourself at the moment instead of getting lost in emotions and sensations.

8. Everybody can be an empath.

This doesn't mean it's something for you and a few other people. Empaths do have wonderful gifts. The real beauty comes from the fact that these gifts aren't limited to a few people. This form of sensitivity is a natural state. With conditioning, beliefs, and upbringings, many of us have lost touch with this state.

Clearing Emotions

Throughout this book, we have talked a lot about energy and emotions. You should be fully aware of the fact that you will absorb a lot of this no matter how hard you try to avoid it. It's a fact for the empath, so it's best to accept. That being said, it's important that you clear out these emotions from time to time. This is something that is called spiritual cleansing. This will help you to improve your gift as well as reduce the risk of negative side effects due to negative emotions. Let's dive right in.

1. Cut the cord

This is important for all empaths since you are great at creating relationships due to the fact that everybody loves you. The problem is, not all of your relationships are good for you and your energy can be sucked out.

The cords of relationships from the past can still exist even if the relationship has ended. You have to cut these cords. In order to do this, visualize the person you have had a relationship with and visualize a cord being sliced. Bless them and say "I release you into the light and love."

There are a lot of advanced techniques to cut the cord, but this is a very easy and simple one you can use. If you complicate it too much, you may find it harder to do.

2. Clear negative thoughts from your aura

Since your energy is constantly mingling with other's energy, sucking up their negative thoughts, you may form thoughts that won't serve your highest purpose. You need to be aware of thoughts that are automatic, repetitive, redundant, and negative.

Carry around a notebook and jot down the thoughts you experience during the day. It will be amazing to see how hard it will be to track thoughts. When you have positive thoughts, they will align with positive vibrations which create harmony, healing, and balance. Negative thoughts cause blockages and resistance.

To clear negativity, look back at your life to notice if you are pulling these bad situations to yourself. If you are, you are vibrating these things into alignment unconsciously. You need to notice your field of energy throughout the day, especially when you start feeling depressed or tired. This will allow you to find out if you have grabbed hold of or created negative thought-forms and then consciously release these.

Picture a silver light cleansing your energy of any thoughts that aren't helping you. This will only take about a minute and can be done multiple times during the day.

3. Smudge your environment and yourself

This is important if you really start to feel down, anxious, or sad. Smudging your environment and yourself helps to remove negative energy. This should be done often, especially when you have been in situations that cause you to feel out of synch. Smudging your house on a regular basis is important too so that the energy their stays fresh.

4. Connect with nature

Everybody who starts to feel overwhelmed, all they have to do is take some time to connect with nature. Nature will cleanse the negative emotions from you. Touch a tree and it will ground you and remove bad energies. Connecting with water, animals, flowers, and the land around you are the most soothing energy therapy. And it's completely free! Take a moment to sit in your yard, against a tree, or take a barefoot walk.

5. Draw, journal, art

Empaths are normally very artistic and love to express their talents. When they aren't feeling great, they will resist their artistic abilities because they require them to feel their feelings and this will cause pain. Art should be used as a form of emotional release that will help you to get yourself unstuck.

6. Cry

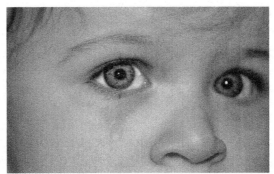

Empaths need to cry often to release emotions. Crying can cleanse your aura.

7. Sea salt bath

Sea salt draws out energy. Taking a warm bath in sea salt is great when you are feeling energetically overwhelmed. Add some essential oils to help release even more.

These are just a few ways to release emotions and you may find other ways that work better for you. What is important is that you take care of yourself and don't allow emotions to remain stagnant inside of you.

Chapter 15: How to Support a Young Empath

An empathic child will have a nervous system that reacts strongly and quickly to external stimulus like stress.

Empathic children feel so much and they don't understand how to manage this sensory overload. They experience more emotions. They have more intuition. They smell, hear, and see more. You might realize they don't like certain smells when you are cooking them dinner. A new perfume might make them sick. They may get headaches in harsh lighting or around loud talking. They like soft clothing, nature, beauty, and having just a few close friends.

Their senses get bombarded by the coarseness of the world and this causes changes to their behavior. Most empathic children don't understand why they get upset. Parents that understand them can help find their triggers and give them solutions to help relieve their stress.

As parents, we need to understand what gets our empathic children over stimulated and stay away from these activities. Doing things that keep them calm will help with anxiety, tantrums, and exhaustion.

Most schools and society don't try to understand these exceptional children. Normal teachers and physicians will label them as fussy, antisocial, or shy. They get diagnosed with depression, anxiety disorder, or social phobia. They tend to be gentle, deep, thoughtful, and quieter instead of being assertive and very verbal. Because they have been wrongly diagnosed, your role as a parent is to support their wisdom, creativity, intuition, and sensitivity. We have to teach them a way to cope with their feelings.

The following things can be done to nurture your empathic child:

1. Encourage their imagination

When you are reading or watching a movie with your child, ask them what they think the person might be feeling or thinking. This will encourage their empathy.

2. Acknowledge other's emotions

Your child needs to understand that everybody's emotions are important and they learn everything from you. Make sure that you respect the emotions of others, so they know their emotions are valid.

3. Play pretend

Playing pretend gets a child ready for real life. This also gives them a chance to play around with different emotions when pretending to be different people.

4. Stick with the feeling

When your child is experiencing a strong emotion, help them work through it. Talk with them to figure out what caused the emotion. This will teach them how to handle it.

Children who are empaths are precious beings. It doesn't matter where your child lands on the spectrum, they would benefit from you teaching them about their sensitivities.

Chapter 16: Exercises You Can do Daily

You've made it this far. You should have a pretty good understanding of your gift and you should be proud that you have it. There have been many different exercises explained throughout this book that you can use to hone into your skills and to make your life easier as an empath. I'm going to leave you with a few more exercises that you can do each day if you want.

With the constant bombardment of negative energy in the world, it can be hard for an empath to remain grounded. Staying at home can even prove to be hard if you keep your empathic antennas turned on. Because of all of these issues, it can be easy for you to become drained, distracted from your roles, and consumed by apathy.

To combat all of this, you have to protect yourself in order to remain grounded. Everyone is different, so what works for one may not work for the other. That said, the best way to protect yourself and remain grounded is to build up a resilience, a strong energy field, a healthy body, and a quiet mind.

1. Diet

Another great thing an empath can do is to include nutritious and grounding foods in their diet and get rid of drug-life foods. Wheat is one of the worst offenders. Empaths are sensitive to vibrations. Everything in the world vibrates at different frequencies and this means alcohol, food, and drugs. Things with low vibrations negatively affect empaths. Most alcohol and drugs will have a low vibration and can bring an empath down.

If you are having a hard time staying grounded, even though you are trying to everything, have a look to see what you are eating.

2. Sea Salt

It's believed that Hippocrates, the father of medicine, was one of the first people to figure out sea salt had healing abilities after he noticed how fast seawater could help a fisherman's wounded hand.

Not only can sea salt heal, but it can also purify. It can remove and dissolve bad energies from your physical and emotional body. You will discover that this is great if you have to interact with people, where it is easy to pick up their anxiety and stress.

3. Exercise

While most people exercise to tone their body and lose weight, exercise can do a lot more for an empath. It is a great way to release pent-up emotions, gets rid of impurities through sweat, improves their mood, increases happiness, energizes, creates an energy field, and is grounding.

Do whatever you love to do. If you don't like following rules or routines, crank up some music and dance like nobody's watching.

4. Creativity

Living in a world of routines and rules, most people don't get time to be creative, but this is the easiest way to get into your feel-good time. When you are feeling good, then you are grounded. When you create things from your passions, it uplifts your psyche. When you are engaging in things that you love, it will keep your mind away from dark feelings and thoughts.

5. Nature

Being around nature is very grounding and healing for empaths. As an empath, if you don't spend all that much time in nature, you are going to struggle to feel grounded and remain balanced.

6. Laughter

Grownups tend to spend way too much time being serious and solemn and too little time having real fun. Can you remember the last time you get to enjoy a really good deep belly laugh? Children laugh all the time. They don't take life seriously as we do. They have fun and play, which helps them to remain grounded. It's important that adults strive to be childlike. To see the wonder in the world and have fun and laugh every now and then. Anything that will make you laugh will help boost your spirits.

7. Crystals

Numerous cultures have been using the healing power of crystals. Ancients used to have crystal chambers that they would use to heal energetic, spiritual, and physical ailments. Crystals can be used along with the chakras to help balance them out and get rid of blockages. Since empaths can naturally sense their healing vibrations, they will be drawn to crystals by their instincts for their protective and grounding abilities.

8. Essential oils

Essential oils work just like crystals in their healing powers and have been used just as long. Through the olfactory senses is where the benefits of oils are obtained. You can find oils that help every empath.

9. Earthing

This may be at the bottom of the list, but it is the most beneficial thing that an empath can do to stay grounded. Earthing means that you place your naked feet on the natural earth, so go for a barefoot walk. The healing power of Mother Earth is often taken for granted, yet it is the easiest way to connect and find balance.

There you go. These exercises can be used every single day to help you stay grounded and connected. Find what works best for you and stick with it.

Conclusion

Thank you for making it through to the end of *Empath Emotional Guide*. Let's hope it was informative and able to provide you with all of the tools you need to achieve your goals whatever they may be.

Being an empath is a wonderful gift. It is nothing to be ashamed of even if it is still misunderstood. Empathic skills can help you and those around you if you know how to use them right. Use the different exercises in this book to help you hone in on your skills. The important thing is to make sure that you take care of yourself and heal yourself.

Finally, if you found this book useful in any way, a review on Amazon is always appreciated!

Enneagram Made Easy

A Spiritual Journey of Self-Discovery to Uncover Your True Personality Type and Become the Healthy Version of Yourself

Introduction

We are excited to take you to this journey of self-discovery to find out which personality type you are and find out new things you never knew about yourself!

Have you been struggling to find your place in this world? Do you question what makes you feel so different from the people around you? Or have you been trying to relate to someone special but just can't seem to find a way to make things "click" with that person?

The answers to these dilemmas and countless others lie in this guide to the Enneagram!

At this point, you might be saying "Any-a-what??!" Or maybe you have already heard of it but you're not sure what it has to do with you. If you are unsure, please be reassured that you have come to the right place! No matter what you're hoping to learn about yourself or other people, help is here.

At first glance, the Enneagram is a symbol. But it's so much more than that! It's a tool for personal transformation and strengthening the ties that bind us together. Millions have witnessed its power to transform lives! People see their own experiences reflected clearly in it and they have had their eyes opened to truths that were right in front of them all along.

The following chapters will discuss everything you need to know about the Enneagram and how to become the best possible version of yourself. You'll learn how to identify your own basic personality type. And you'll learn how to use that information to grow personally, improve relationships and your work life, and relate to others on a profound level.

The nine personality types are: Reformer, Peacemaker, Challenger, Helper, Achiever, Individualist, Investigator, Loyalist, and Enthusiast. Perhaps you can already guess what your type might be by name alone. Prepare to be completely blown away when you learn your true type and what it means.

There are plenty of books on this subject on the market, so thanks again for choosing this one! Every effort was made to ensure it is full of as much useful information as possible. Please enjoy!

Part 1: Getting Our Feet Wet, Enneagram Style

Chapter 1: The Enneagram – What Is It and How Do We Use It?

A Brief History of the Enneagram

To understand the Enneagram, it might help you to know a bit about where it came from. The word Enneagram comes from the Greek words *ennea*, which means "nine," and *gramma*, meaning "model," "points," or something "written" or "drawn."

The early origins of Enneagram are greatly disputed and not officially known. Some claim that the symbol originated in the ancient mathematics of the Pythagoreans, some 4000 years ago. Others believe that the philosopher Philo introduced a version of the Enneagram to esoteric Judaism, where it later became a part of the Tree of Life in the Kabbalah discipline. Still, others believe it originated in Islamic Sufi mysticism. It also seems to include aspects of ancient mystical Christianity, Taoism, Buddhism, and Greek philosophy.

The Enneagram's modern form and use are credited to a few specific sources. George Gurdjieff, a Greek-Armenian spiritual teacher, used the Enneagram symbol to explain the laws of creation and aspects of the universe. He probably first saw the symbol when he visited a monastery in Afghanistan during the 1920s.

The current system of Enneagram personality typing started with Oscar Ichazo, who founded a school of self-realization in Chile in the 1950s and 60s. He developed the basic principles of Enneagram theory from ideas of early Christianity, mystical Judaism, and classic Greek philosophies. A student of Ichazo in 1970 was psychiatrist Claudio Naranjo, who brought the Enneagram to the U.S. Its popularity spread throughout North America within a few years.

In 1973, an American teacher named Don Riso added insights from modern psychology to Enneagram teachings. In 1988, Russ Hudson joined him and they developed the personality typing system of today. After continually experiencing its power as a tool for understanding ourselves and those around us, Riso and Hudson formed The Enneagram Institute in 1997 to further research and development. Currently, the institute develops and sponsors workshops and training so the power of the Enneagram can keep improving human lives.

An observation that modern psychological research has made about the Enneagram is its incredible accuracy in terms of insights into human nature. Not only does it confirm what has already been discovered about the psyche, but it can also anticipate the knowledge found in modern psychological diagnostic tools.

In short, the Enneagram has ancient and mysterious origins, but its modern personality typing is very impressive!

The Enneagram's Shape

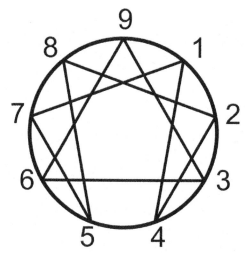

Without the elegantly simple geometric shape of the Enneagram, we would not have a thorough understanding of the nine basic personality types and how they interconnect and relate to each other. So let's take a look at it for a moment.

On the outside is a circle with nine points spread equally around the circle. It's important that all nine personality types are connected in the circle because a human being has the potential for any of these personalities.

On each side of a type lies another potential type, and these are called *wings*. For example, the wings of type 7 are the numbers 6 and 8. Although you may be a type 7, you may lean heavily towards either 6 or 8 – this leaning is called your wing. You'll learn about this in Chapter 2.

Inside the circle is an equilateral triangle (all three sides of equal length), which connects the points 3, 6, and 9. The second shape inside the circle is an irregular hexagonal figure (six-sided figure with unequal sides) that connects the rest of the points in this order: 1-4-2-8-5-7-1. This order will become important in Chapter 2 when we discuss *directions of integration and disintegration.*

Notice the placement of the numbers one through nine. On the left side are numbers 5, 6, and 7. On the top are 8, 9, and 1. On the right are 2, 3, and 4. The 9 types are divided into three groups called triads. Within each triad, the three personality types have a dominant emotion in common. Learning more about the triad that your personality stems from will give you further valuable insight into your personality and help you on your path to self-awareness.

What Sets The Enneagram Apart?

You've probably seen a lot of personality tests. But the Enneagram is not just a test. It's a conceptualization of the human experience. It explains how all types are connected. It tells *why* we think, act, and feel certain ways instead of just *how* we think, act, and feel.

All those personality tests may tell you what you are likely to do in certain situations or how you may feel when faced with certain situations. But wouldn't it be nice to understand the *why* behind those thoughts and actions?

The Enneagram teachings are the first of any personality typing systems to reveal the basic primal instincts, fears, and survival mechanisms that drive us to become who we are. It's a tool for not only understanding your personality but for unlocking the potential for growth within yourself. By understanding how you became who you are and what drives you, you can conquer fears holding you back and cope with negative emotions that you previously tried to avoid.

The Enneagram is important as a spiritual tool. Whether you have a strong faith in one God or believe in the broader, innate spirituality of the universe, you can use what you learn to find spiritual enlightenment. Unlike many psychological tools, the teachings of the Enneagram address character defects. It helps us understand how we can be held captive to our fears and basic passions. It aids us in finding ways to rise above our character defects. Consequently, you learn where you need spiritual healing and discover how to reach this healing.

Enneagram is also an important tool for interacting with other people in your life! Whether you want to understand your business associates, enhance your romantic relationship, or improve your parenting style, you can find the answers here. By gaining insights into the motivations of others, you can learn how to interact with them harmoniously. So keep reading!

How to Read this Book

You do not have to read this entire book word-for-word if you don't want to. It may be helpful and interesting for some people to read the whole thing. But you may prefer to just read about your own type and the types of a few key people in your life. It's up to you!

However, we do recommend that you stick with us for another couple of chapters first. In Chapter 2, you'll learn what it means to have a basic personality type and how to get the most out of learning about your specific type. Then, in Chapter 3, you'll get to determine your most likely personality type out of the 9.

Chapters 4 through 12 each cover a specific personality type, so here's where you can jump around as much as you please. You can just go to your specific type, or maybe, you'll want to read about your possible wings as well. At the end of each chapter, you'll get relationship hints for each type.

Chapter 2: The Basic Personality Type

The Nine Types

You'll read in-depth descriptions of each personality types in later chapters, but here are some very brief descriptions. Some authors call these personalities by alternate names. Here, they are listed by the Riso-Hudson type names (so named after the two founders of The Enneagram Institute):

- **Type 1:** The Reformer – self-controlled, rational, principled, and perfectionist.

- **Type 2:** The Helper – caring, generous, genuine, people-pleasing, and possessive.

- **Type 3:** The Achiever – competitive, success-oriented, appearance-driven, and focused.

- **Type 4:** The Individualist – sensitive, expressive, creative, unique, dramatic, temperamental, and romantic.

- **Type 5:** The Investigator – innovative, curious, perceptive, quiet, withdrawn, and careful.

- **Type 6:** The Loyalist – responsible, anxious, committed, trustworthy, and suspicious.

- **Type 7:** The Enthusiast – versatile, optimistic, social, adventurous, impulsive, and distractible.

- **Type 8:** The Challenger – decisive, confident, dominating, independent, intense, and confrontational.

- **Type 9:** The Peacemaker – reassuring, accommodating, easygoing, supportive, complacent, and avoids conflicts.

Inside you lay the potential for all these personality types. That is why you may be able to relate to many or even all of them. However, as you take the test and keep reading, one of them should seem closest to your true nature. This one type is your *basic personality type.*

Which type becomes your dominant personality is influenced by several things. Before you are born, genetics affect the ways you are likely to think, feel, and act. Although environmental factors that influence you after birth are important, most experts agree that your dominant type was determined before you were born.

After birth, your basic personality type continued to be shaped by outside influences. Your environment and the way that you were raised played a huge part in shaping your *defense mechanisms*, which are important parts of your personality type. Everyone learns to behave and react to their environment differently, and we all leave childhood with a unique view of the world.

Before going further, there are a couple of important things to understand. Even though the types are represented by numbers, no personality is more important or better than any other personality. It's okay if you don't relate to every part of the description of your dominant personality type. We all fluctuate regularly in spiritual and emotional health, and you will relate more to some traits than others at various times in your life. *However*, no one ever changes from one principal type of personality to another. Not ever.

The Triads

As you read in the previous chapter, the nine personalities are divided into three sets of three groups called triads. The chapters about the personalities are grouped by these triads. The triads are called the *Instinctive* Triad, the *Feeling* Triad, and the *Thinking* Triad. Within each triad, the three basic personality types have specific underlying emotions in common.

This book is organized so that the three Triads are grouped together, so the order of the nine personalities is as follows: 8, 9, 1, 2, 3, 4, 5, 6, and 7.

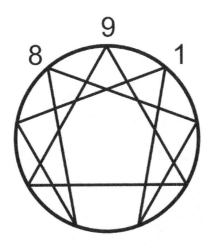

The Instinctive Triad – Types 8, 9, and 1

For the three personalities, anger is the dominant emotion in the Instinctive Triad. Each of the personalities deals with their anger differently. When an Eight feels anger, they tend to act on it almost immediately in a physical way, such as yelling or acting aggressively. In contrast, a Nine denies their anger and focuses on the other people in their lives. Ones try to control their anger and often turn it inwards upon themselves.

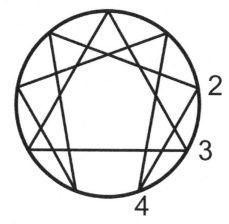

The Feeling Triad – Types 2, 3, and 4

In the Feeling Triad, your dominant emotion is *shame*. A type Two tries to make up for their feelings of shame by people-pleasing (attempts to get others to like and want them). Threes deal with underlying shame by denying it and trying to become the opposite of a shameful person through constant achievement and success. A Four avoids shame by focusing on theirs and by creating a kind of fantasy life to ignore any ordinary parts of their life.

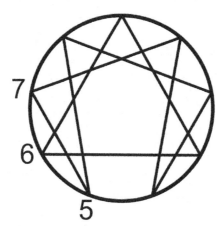

The Thinking Triad – Types 5, 6, and 7

The third triad deals with *anxiety*. Type Five suffers from anxiety about dealing with the outside world, and they cope by withdrawing from the world. A Six can be highly anxious, especially when it comes to trusting their own minds and instincts. They can succumb to this anxiety at times, but some Sixes may suddenly confront their fear and defy it. Sevens have fears about their inner negative emotions, like pain and loss. They deal with it by avoiding negative emotions and seeking stimulating activity and many distractions.

Traps, Avoidances, Idealizations, and Core Beliefs

In the description of each basic personality type, you'll read about *traps, avoidances, and idealizations*. To avoid confusion later, we'll define and explain these terms now.

Each personality type of the Enneagram has a *trap* – some focus or obsession that keeps you from making personal progress and growing spiritually. For example, a type One can be so obsessed with perfection and making things right that they are not able to see beyond their own self-imposed standards.

Avoidances are feelings and ideas that members of each personality type do their very best to avoid at all costs. Essentially, avoidances are our deep fears. A type Three will go to great lengths to avoid feeling like a failure while the behavior of type Seven is centered around avoiding any kind of emotional pain. These avoidances are closely linked to the traps defined in the paragraph above. Our avoidances are things that we need to experience growth.

Idealizations are the images that each personality type tries to present to the world, the standard that their behavior is focused on living up to, or what they believe to be the most important trait a person can exhibit. For example, an Eight does their best to project an image of strength, so their idealization is "I am a strong person."

Your traps, avoidances, and idealizations exist because of your basic personality type's *core belief* system. Your core belief is your perspective of the world, the filter through which you experience life and prioritize what you believe are the most desirable traits and behaviors. Our core beliefs are usually unconscious, so we are not aware of their influence on our personalities.

Wrapping your head around all of these traits of the different personality types can take a little practice, but it will begin to make more sense as you read about your own type and realize how accurately your experiences are described in your type's chapter.

Vices/Passions

Each type's unique characteristics lead them to have unique weaknesses, which many experts list under the labels of *vices or passions*. These are the tendencies that can hinder our spiritual growth and lead us astray from the more noble characteristics of our types. An example of this can be seen in Eights, who sometimes, have the passion of lust. This isn't necessarily sexual lust; rather, it is a term for *intensity*. Eights crave the feeling of being fully alive. They tend to fully engage and exert their influence in everything they do. However, this intensity can be too aggressive and overwhelming.

Wings

Earlier, we mentioned *wings*, which are the numbers on either side of each personality type. While you may have one dominant personality type, no one's traits ever fall entirely into one category. Most people find that they are a mix of their dominant personality type plus one of the two types on either side. If you are a Five, you may find that you also identify with many characteristics of either Four or Six.

Your wing type adds important elements to your overall personality. Sometimes, these wing traits complement those of your dominant type, and sometimes, they are even in opposition to each other. It is very important to study the wing type so that you can truly gain a better understanding of yourself or another person that you are learning about.

Levels of Development

Another factor of personality types that make each individual unique is the *levels of development* within each type. This may seem complicated and confusing at first glance, but it's important to discuss because your personality's levels of development are critical to the personal growth you desire!

In each type is nine levels of development (don't confuse this with the nine dominant types!). Just like the triads, these levels come in three sets of three. The healthy range, average range, and the unhealthy range all have three development levels:

You'll learn more about the levels of each type in the specific chapters.

	Level 1	The Level of Liberation
Healthy	Level 2	The Level of Psychological Capacity
	Level 3	The Level of Social Value
	Level 4	The Level of Imbalance/ Social Role
Average	Level 5	The Level of Interpersonal Control
	Level 6	The Level of Overcompensation
	Level 7	The Level of Violation
Unhealthy	Level 8	The Level of Obsession and Compulsion
	Level 9	The Level of Pathological Destructiveness

By learning about your personality type, you will make a start at becoming healthier. Recognizing how your personality shapes your worldview is a first step in becoming more and aware of yourself, your thoughts, and your environment. Countless people have learned that the more they learn about their dominant type, the more they can free themselves of damaging emotions and beliefs and see themselves accurately.

Just imagine what your own personal growth experience might be once you have learned about your type and begin to make progress!

Directions of Disintegration (Stress) and Integration (Growth)

As we noted in the description of the Enneagram's structure, the nine points are not connected at random but in a very specific pattern. The order of connection represents how each type of person tends to behave under different circumstances.

The points on the equilateral triangle are 3, 6, and 9. In a clockwise direction, the sequence is 9-3-6-9. This is the direction of integration, and it shows how individuals behave in times of healthy personal growth. For example, a healthy Three under secure conditions will display some of the characteristics of a Six.

In the opposite direction, the order of the triangle is 9-6-3-9, and this is the direction of disintegration or stress. It shows how a person will behave in particularly stressful situations. For example, an average Nine under long-term stress will behave more like an average Six, and an unhealthy Three under stressful conditions will begin to act like an unhealthy Nine.

Integration Arrows

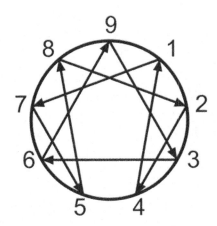

The remaining six points form an irregular hexagon with overlapping lines that cannot be followed in a clockwise or counter-clockwise direction. However, they do have a specific Direction of Integration (Growth): 1-7-5-8-2-4-1. And they have a Direction of Disintegration (Stress): 1-4-2-8-5-7-1. As with the triangle, these directions show how people of each type behave during times of personal growth or under conditions of long-term stress.

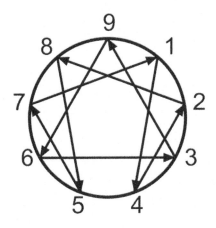

Disintegration Arrows

These Directions of Integration and Disintegration are not just theoretical! They have been observed by psychologists and Enneagram teachers time and again as they work with individuals of each of the nine different types. As you think back on your own experiences, you may be able to better understand your past behaviors under stressful conditions or during times of healthy personal growth.

Instinctual Variants, a.k.a. "Subtypes"

One more thing that makes us each unique is our *three basic instincts*. These are in each human being and are almost as necessary to life as breathing oxygen. These are the *social instinct* (for forming bonds with other people and social structure in a community), the *sexual instinct* (for forming one-to-one bonds and reproducing), and the *self-*

preservation instinct (this is the instinct we use especially for needs and threats to preserve our own life and body.)

Your personality affects how you react to these instincts and how you prioritize each of the three needs. In turn, the three basic instincts also affect the way that your personality expresses itself. Each of us tends to prioritize only one instinct. This is called our *dominant instinct or subtype*. With the possibility of three different dominant instincts within each of the nine personality types, there are really twenty-seven possible combinations of personality type and dominant instinct. Add to those twenty-seven combinations are the possible wing types and levels of development, and there are a lot of unique personalities!

If you think about all you've learned so far, you'll see that the Enneagram shows how fluid and connected all the personalities really are. Your behavior can change based on whether you are in stressful conditions or conditions that encourage spiritual growth. Your psychological health can change, causing you to move up or down the levels of development within your personality type. And your wing personality type can express itself at times while remaining hidden at others. If you had any concerns about whether Enneagram's personality typing would label you or "put you in a box," hopefully, you can now see that the opposite is true. With the help of the Enneagram, you can unlock knowledge about the complexity and fluidity of your personality and discover secrets to your mind's inner workings – and the inner workings of the important people in your life!

Chapter 3: What's Your Number? The Type Quiz

This is a short quiz to help you determine your basic personality type. There are longer, more in-depth tests available, for a fee, from various sources online and in print. After scoring your quiz, we recommend that recommended that you read the chapters about your top three types in the next part of this book.

Instructions for the Quiz:

Get a spare piece of paper and write out numbers 1 through 36. For each number (starting on the next page), write the letter next to the statement that is most true for you. If a statement such as " It has often been easy for other people to upset me," for example, seems to describe you better than "It has typically taken quite a lot for other people to upset me," write down the letter of that statement.

Keep in mind that for each number, both statements may have described you at one point or another in isolated incidents. However, think about which statement describes you more accurately in general and most often in the past.

When taking this type of quiz, it has often helped people to think of how they behaved in their early 20s. Remember that this quiz is about your gut reactions and behavior, not occasional feelings or times that you have been influenced by others.

Remember that there are no "right" answers and no personality type is better than any other. Each one has its own virtues and temptations. Also, this test doesn't determine whether you are psychologically healthy or unhealthy. Just answer the questions honestly and quickly, without over-analyzing the meaning behind the answers. Be as spontaneous as you can in answering.

Someone who knows you very well can also help you discover your personality in case there is a tie in your scores. It usually takes ten minutes or less to finish the quiz. Instructions for scoring and determining your type are at the end of the quiz.

Also, remember that this fun and short personality quiz is not scientifically based. Many factors can influence your results, so they are not guaranteed.

The Enneagram Type Indicator Quiz

*For each question, below, choose **ONE** of the two statements. Record the letters representing your answers on a spare sheet of paper. (for example, for number 1, record letter "A" if the first statement describes you better and "F" if the second statement describes you more closely)*

1. G. I am afraid of getting too involved with people, because it may lead to conflict or confrontation.

2.
- B. I am afraid of not being involved enough with people, because I want them to depend on me heavily.

2.
- F. I have great knowledge of some subjects, which has been helpful to others at times.
- E. I have great strength and can make decisions in a crisis, which has been helpful to others at times.

3.
- F. For the most part, I am usually intensely focused on the task at hand and unwilling to change my plans.
- H. For the most part, I am usually looking for the next fun thing and willing to change my plans at a moments' notice.

4.
- C. It has often been easy for other people to upset me.
- G. It has typically taken quite a lot for anyone to upset me.

5.
- E. I like to take charge of situations and provide the strength that others need.
- D. I like to do the best I possibly can in every situation, and often my best feels like it isn't good enough.

6.
- E. I have learned to be strong by surviving many challenges that life has thrown at me.
- D. I have high ideals of proper behavior for myself and others, and I am disappointed when these ideals are not met.

7.
- B. I enjoy being emotionally and physically intimate with people, openly showing affection when possible.
- F. I enjoy keeping my distance from people, and I do not blend well with others.

8.
- B. I tend to focus more on fostering friendships than accomplishments.
- I. I tend to focus more on fostering accomplishments than friendships.

9.
- I. I have been opportunistic, only welcoming new experiences if they will benefit me.
- H. I have been a fun-seeker, only welcoming new experiences if they seem exciting.

10.
- A. I have typically been too self-centered, often not noticing other people.
- G. I have typically moved the focus away from me and onto others too much.

11.
- A. I have usually had a good imagination and have often over-dramatized situations in my head.

	C.	I have usually viewed situations from a practical and realistic point of view.
12.	C.	I have tended to lack confidence in myself.
	D.	I have tended to be over-confident in myself.
13.	I.	I have typically been able to compartmentalize my feelings and focus on the task at hand.
	A.	If I have strong feelings, I have typically needed to sort through these emotions before I can focus on anything else.
14.	A.	I have felt misunderstood and alone, unwilling to speak my mind.
	G.	I have been typically brave enough to say things that others wish they could.
15.	I.	I am usually able to further my ambitions by attracting people with my charm and diplomacy.
	D.	I am usually unable to be particularly charming; because of my high moralistic ideals, I prefer a more formal and direct approach to people.
16.	F.	I have had a very difficult time being decisive.
	D.	I have been very decisive, and have had a difficult time allowing for any flexibility in my ideas.
17.	B.	I love to welcome new friends into my life with open arms and hospitality.
	A.	I have trouble mixing with others, and I keep my personal thoughts to myself.
18.	C.	I think through things carefully and approach tasks one step at a time.
	H.	I tend to "leap before I look," preferring adventure to caution.
19.	B.	I truly enjoy being around others and lending a helping hand.
	D.	I take a fairly serious approach to life and prefer to discuss the morality of issues.
20.	F.	I am most interested in being independent and seeking facts.
	G.	I am most interested in keeping peace and stability in my environment.
21.	E.	I have often been quick to confront others.
	G.	I have often avoided confrontations at all costs.
22.	H.	When I make a commitment, I fear that I am missing out on something better.
	E.	When I get close to someone, I fear letting down my guard.

23. C. I tend to be very hesitant to make commitments.

    E. I tend to be very bold, to the point of over-powering those around me.

24. A. I tend to keep myself apart from others.

    E. I tend to be somewhat bossy.

25. G. If something in my world is not at peace, I tend to numb myself to the problem with some comforting activity.

    H. If something in my world is not at peace, I tend to indulge myself in some sort of treat.

26. C. I like to choose friends that I can trust implicitly, and they can expect the same from me.

    I. I do not like to depend on people; I prefer to be self-sufficient.

27. F. I have tended to be distracted and absent-minded.

    A. I have tended to be dramatic and emotional.

28. E. I enjoy a healthy debate among friends.

    B. I enjoy being a source of comfort and support for friends.

29. H. I am usually extroverted and eager to enjoy activities with others.

    D. I am usually very disciplined and strive to follow the rules.

30. A. I do not like drawing attention to myself.

    I. I like showing off and getting attention for my talents.

31. F. I am more interested in acquiring knowledge than worldly materials.

    C. I am more interested in being sure of my security than in pursuing any hobbies or passions.

32. A. In disagreements with others, I like to escape into my own private thoughts and fantasies.
    E. In disagreements with others, I like to be confrontational.

33. G. I tend to be a "pushover" to keep the peace.

    D. I tend to have high expectations of others, and I do not compromise these expectations easily.

34. H. I have a quick wit and optimistic attitude.

    B. I am a truly supportive and generous friend.

35. I. I am great at impressing people I have just met.

    F. I am great at displaying my knowledge in my chosen field of interest.

36. C. I have been known as a skeptic, rarely or never swayed by emotions.

    B. I have been known to be sentimental and easily swayed by emotions.

Scoring Your Quiz:

Add the number of each of the letters (A through I) you have on your piece of paper. If you have taken the quiz correctly and chosen one statement for each question, 36 should be the total of all of the numbers added together. If this is not your total, check your answers or your arithmetic again.

Each type of personality is represented by letters as shown below. Take note that *they are not in numerical order and are randomized*:

A = Type 4 (The Individualist)

B = Type 2 (The Helper)

C = Type 6 (The Loyalist)

D = Type 1 (The Reformer)

E = Type 8 (The Challenger)

F = Type 5 (The Investigator)

G = Type 9 (The Peacemakor)

H = Type 7 (The Enthusiast)

I = Type 3 (The Achiever)

The goal of the quiz is to discover your basic personality type out of the nine types. Answering the questions accurately and honestly will give you your type based on the top three scores. The following chapters include the description of each type. Check them out so that you can confirm your results.

Further resources will be given at the end of this book so that you can continue your research!

You can still review and double-check your answers if you got unclear results, or read about the different types so you can decide which ones most closely resembles your personality.

Part 2: Diving In - Learning About the Types

Please note that this book is organized so that the three Triads are grouped together, so the order of the nine personalities is as follows: 8, 9, 1, 2, 3, 4, 5, 6, and 7. For a review of what the personalities in each Triad have in common, please refer back to Chapter 2.

The Instinctive Triad (Types 8, 9 & 1)

Chapter 4: Type 8 – The Challenger

Type 8 Checklist: *How many of the following statements are true for you?*

- You are confident in yourself and assertive.
- You "shoot from the hip" when you speak.
- You are often the first to take charge of a situation.
- You are resourceful and decisive.
- You have protective instincts.
- You have a big heart and like to "take people under your wing."
- You feel you must control your environment, including the people around you.
- You can become self-centered and dominate or intimidate people.
- You sometimes have trouble controlling your temper.
- You fear to be vulnerable or controlled.
- You can inspire people and improve their lives with your strength.
- You want a lot out of life and feel prepared to go out and get it.
- You want to be financially independent and can have trouble working for someone else.
- You have a hard time trusting anyone right away.
- You have a strong sense of right and wrong and a strong desire for truth and justice.

If you can relate to more than half of the above statements, chances are that you are an Eight or you have a strong Eight wing. Keep reading to learn more about your type!
Core Belief

The belief that drives your behavior is that the world is an unjust place in which weak or innocent people are taken advantage of. Only the strong survive!

Avoidance: *Weakness*

You avoid weakness and being vulnerable. This avoidance highlights your basic fear of being controlled by others; you feel that if you expose any vulnerability, others might use that vulnerability to control you in some way.

Trap: *Enforcing Justice*

You can become so preoccupied with enforcing justice and/or protecting those around you that you are not focused on where you need to develop personally and spiritually.

Idealization: *I am strong.*

This is the image that you wish to project to the world. Doing so helps you avoid the thing you fear, appearing vulnerable.

Defense Mechanism: *Denial*

Denial is the refusal to accept certain realities, thoughts, or feelings. You use denial to protect the sensitivity and vulnerability underneath your tough outer surface of strength and control. If you feel a hint of weakness or powerlessness, you kill those emotions with the powerful defense mechanism of denial.

Passion: *Lust* (Intensity)

As a person who values physical strength, you want to feel intensely alive. You want to be fully engaged in life, and you don't appreciate people who only go through the motions. This can be good, but your intensity can become aggression, which overwhelms and intimidates others.

Description

You enjoy taking on challenges, and you like to challenge others through encouragement for them to improve their abilities. Sometimes, you also challenge authority. You have strong protective instincts for the people who are close to you. You stand up for what is right and speak your mind when you feel that justice is not being served.

As a member of the *Instinctive Triad*, your emotional issues center on anger, which you act on quickly in a physical way, such as speaking forcefully, yelling, or acting aggressively. Even if you are not violent or physically harmful, your forceful expressions of anger can be frightening to some people.

You are a natural leader. You excel at taking charge and getting things done. Many people find you to be a good leader because your strong sense of justice leads you to treat everyone fairly. However, at times, you can become domineering and intimidating.

You have strong willpower and seemingly unlimited energy, which contribute to your natural charisma. You also use these qualities to keep people from hurting you. From childhood, you learned to keep people at arm's length and display strength. You feel that being in charge and being strong will protect you from emotional pain.

Wings

The personalities to either side of you on the Enneagram are Seven, the Enthusiast, and Nine, the Peacemaker. An Eight with a stronger Seven-Wing has been labeled "The Maverick" by some, and Eight with a stronger Nine-Wing has been labeled "The Bear." Read the chapters on these personalities to decide if you identify more strongly with one of these wings.

Directions of Integration and Disintegration

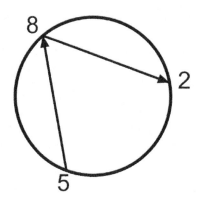

Your direction of integration is towards type Two, the Helper. This means that when you are emotionally healthy, you exhibit qualities of a healthy Two. When you recognize that your tough outer shell isolates you from others and begin opening yourself up to a few, others discover your generosity and warmth. You want to express your love and support for the people in your world.

If you are less emotionally healthy but in secure conditions, you may display the traits of an average Two. You can show your emotional side to a few people who are very close to you while still appearing strong and impervious in public. You may also become somewhat manipulative (like an average or unhealthy Two) as you try to hold on to the people who are close to you.

Your direction of disintegration is towards type Five, the Investigator. Your first reaction to stress as an Eight is to tackle the immediate challenge. However, you may eventually become overwhelmed by the effort. If you become too stressed, you might retreat from your usual aggressive approach and isolate yourself. This can help you to assess the problem, but if it lasts for too long or the stress is too great you may become colder and more cynical, like unhealthy Fives.

Levels of Development

The following is a very brief breakdown of your levels of development as an Eight, so you can begin to recognize your psychological health and warning signs of emotional deterioration.

- **Healthy**
    - **Level 1 (at your best):** You restrain yourself well and show mercy. You submit to leadership. You are a loyal friend and you sacrifice yourself for loved ones. You are emotionally open. You do not need to constantly assert yourself or control anyone. You have heroic qualities.
    - **Level 2:** You are resourceful and self-starting, with a passion that keeps you going. You stand up for what you need. You are confident and assertive, not intimidating.
    - **Level 3:** Others look up to you as a leader. You show honor in protecting and helping others.

- **Average**
    - **Level 4:** You are a hard worker. You strive to accomplish your goals of independence. You deny your own emotional needs.
    - **Level 5:** You need to feel others' support. You forcefully try to control your environment and expect to be obeyed. Your pride keeps you from respecting others.
    - **Level 6:** You use force and intimidation to get your way, sometimes, resorting to threats. You are confrontational. People may resent you for your disrespect.

- **Unhealthy**
    - **Level 7:** You are ruthless, possibly violent. You have no sympathy for others and will sacrifice morals to get your way. You defy any and all authority.
    - **Level 8:** You feel invincible, impervious, and omnipotent. You are obsessed with your own power.
    - **Level 9:** You are dangerously destructive, potentially sociopathic. Possible Antisocial Personality Disorder.

Subtypes/Instincts

If you are a *social* Eight, you value friendship. You are extremely loyal and willing to make great sacrifices for your friends, and you expect the same from them. You enjoy friendly debates, and you love expressing your opinion in a controversial manner. This trait can be a turn-off to others, but you don't understand why. You enjoy being surrounded by friends and seek others who have strength and independence. If you are psychologically unhealthy, you may often make promises to your friends and not follow through.

As a *sexual* Eight, you can be intense in your relationships. You seek to feel fully alive when you are with your love interests. You want your partner to be strong enough that you can open yourself up, but you may become too domineering in your efforts to form them into the person you want them to be. You enjoy feeling challenged by your partner, but you may become arguments.

Finally, if you are a *self-preservation* Eight, you prioritize the accumulation of resources as a means to independence. You may be a skilled business person. You are resourceful and able to see your way out of most difficult situations, and you are most likely an excellent provider. Others in your household may resent the control you exert over the house resources.

Psychological and Spiritual Growth

An important key to growth as an Eight is to recognize that you do not need to constantly defy the world or view life as a battle of wills. Begin to understand that true strength is found in the ability to open yourself emotionally and express vulnerability. This openness attracts more people.

You have suppressed your innocence because you believe it makes you weak and vulnerable. Learn to reclaim that innocence by appreciating the simplicity and expressing gratitude for small blessings.

Embrace your natural leadership abilities but understand that cooperation will yield more positive results than attempts to bend people to your will. Learn to use less force and appreciate the individualities of people around you.

Notice when you feel vulnerable and out of control, and instead of denying those feelings, accept them. Start by discussing the feelings that make you feel vulnerable with someone you trust. Realize that you most likely will not be met with ridicule or disgust. You are at your most honest and attractive when you can admit to being human. Practice this a little at a time.

Take the experience of a type Eight college campus minister who is learning to harness her overpowering tendencies. Because of Enneagram teachings, she has recently learned to be more aware of her desire to be in control. She explains that, by learning more about her type, she has gained the ability to recognize when she is pushing too hard to advance her own desires.

Thanks to her Enneagram learning and growth experience, this Eight, who is blessed with the strong leadership abilities of most Eights, understands that true leadership means knowing when to give up her agenda for the greater good. She now strives to challenge students on campus to accomplish things for their own good, not just for what she thinks they should do.

Relationships

This section consists of helpful hints *for* Eights in relationships and for people in relationships *with* Eights. These include business relationships, romantic relationships, and parent-child relationships.

Business Relationships FOR *Eights:*
- Learn to respect the individual strengths of others, including those who seem weak.
- Understand that "might makes right" is not necessarily true.
- Decide how much force is needed in each situation.
- Recognize differences between advancing your own agenda and doing what is best for the business.
- Listen to and consider the contributions of others.
- Show appreciation for others.
- Submit to those in authority above you; be respectful when raising concerns or disagreements.
- Be patient, even with those who seem slow or incompetent to you.

Business Relationships WITH *Eights:*
- Make direct eye contact and be assertive.
- Do not disrespect them or try to control them.
- Let them help you get things moving.
- In disagreements, stand up to them and confront them directly.
- Accept their energy but challenge them to rein it in.
- Confront them on destructive or threatening behavior and understand that they may be covering for feelings of vulnerability.

Parenting FOR *Eights:*
- Embrace your instincts to be loyal, protective, involved, and devoted.
- Don't be overprotective; your children need to learn to make mistakes.
- Recognize when you may be too rigid or demanding. Seek the opinion of your co-parent or other parents if you are uncertain. This may feel too vulnerable, but it's good for you!
- Practice patience.

Parenting When Your CHILD *Is an Eight*
- Encourage their independence and fighting spirit if it isn't rebellious or dangerous.
- Don't get in a battle of wills. Explain that you refuse to argue.
- Model submission to authority (the law, your boss, etc.) so your child understands its necessity.
- Watch for manipulation and show that it does not work for you.
- Do not necessarily be concerned if your child is a loner, but encourage him or her to look for things they appreciate and admire in their peers.
- Be a model of expressing vulnerability and emotional openness. Reward this with respect and affection.

Romantic Relationships FOR *Eights:*
- Listen to your partner's point of view.
- Tell your partner regularly what you are thankful for them being with you.
- Get feedback for how forcefully you come across.
- Learn to open emotionally. Start in small ways and build.
- Explain when you don't feel safe and allow for reassurance.
- Find an activity (separate from your partner) where you can safely release the anger that is kept within you.
- Practice patience.
- Resist the urge to be possessive.

Romantic Relationships WITH *Eights:*
- Notice any time they open emotionally and reward this with respect and affection.
- Show appreciation for times when they make sacrifices for you, show extra loyalty or commitment.
- Be direct with them when you have anything to discuss.
- Stand up to them when you feel they seem to be controlling or talking down to you.
- Remind them they don't have to carry the weight of the world on their shoulders.

Chapter 5: Type 9 – The Peacemaker

Type 9 Checklist: *Ask yourself if the following statements are true for you.*

- You are generally patient and easygoing.
- You are receptive and agreeable when hearing the ideas of others.
- You think of yourself as uncomplicated and contented.
- You have been accused of being unrealistic in the way that you idealize people and the way that the world should work.
- You are not usually self-conscious.
- You are a steady and supportive friend.
- You can be very imaginative and creative.
- You prefer to "keep the peace" rather than show when you are upset.
- You sometimes escape into distraction to deal with tension or neglect.
- Occasionally, you have "blown up" after absorbing too much abuse and holding it in for too long.
- You have difficulty standing up for yourself and voicing your own feelings.
- You prefer to keep your life simple and stick to a few close friends and family members.
- You want to believe the best in people and hope for the best for yourself.
- You would rather avoid a problem than confront it head-on.
- You make an excellent mediator in conflicts.

If you can relate to more than half of the above statements, chances are that you are a Nine or you have a strong Nine wing. Keep reading to learn more about your type!

Core Belief

The belief that drives your behavior is that you have to always go with the flow or blend in so that you feel valued and loved. You believe that the world would be a better place if everyone just treated each other more respectfully and tried to get along.

Avoidance: *Conflict*

You avoid the discomfort of conflict at all costs. You fear "rocking the boat" because it may lead to loss and separation, and as a result, you often deny your needs and desires.

Trap: *Being Temperate*

You can become so preoccupied with making peace and/or avoiding conflict that you end up repressing powerful feelings within you.

Idealization: *I am harmonious.*

By appearing harmonious and keeping the peace, you protect yourself from the pain of being dismissed or hurt by the ones you love.

Defense Mechanism: *Narcotization*

Narcotization is "numbing out" to deal with negative feelings, and it is a common defense mechanism in Nines. You may use TV or other technology, repetitive thinking patterns, comfort food, alcohol, or even drugs to stop feeling any painful emotions. Even seemingly productive activity can be a type of narcotization if it keeps you from facing your emotions.

Passion: *Sloth* (Disengagement)

You pay a large price for the relaxed, harmonious image that you project. Because you spend so much of your emotional energy suppressing anger and frustration with other people (and with yourself), you feel fatigued much of the time. You feel that you have no more energy left to spend, so you end up being disengaged from life. This sloth is not necessarily a quality of laziness, even if it may appear so to others.

Description

You seek to achieve and maintain a sense of peace in your world, both externally and internally. You prefer to create harmony in your environment.

You are usually able to see multiple points of view in a conflict. This makes you an excellent mediator, which people value in your personal life and in the business world.

Sometimes, you have trouble staying on task or prioritizing what needs to be done. You're an excellent "big picture" thinker, but you may need help seeing the details. Short-term objectives work best for you.

You struggle to focus on disturbing or negative issues, and you just want to avoid them instead. Dealing with conflict in your environment has been learned as a child by being undemanding and withdrawing. As an adult, you are un-demanding and non-judgmental, and these qualities draw people to you and make you a supportive friend.

As a member of the *Instinctive Triad*, you have issues with anger, which you deal with by denying it and focusing on creating peace for the other people in your life instead. You are usually unaware of any repressed anger inside you, but sometimes, it comes out explosively. If you are surrounded by tense conditions or frustrated with the behavior of people around you, you may eventually reach a boiling point and erupt. Afterward, you hope to just keep going as if "everything is ok."

One of the best qualities about you is your optimism. You want to believe in the best about other people and hope for the best for yourself. You may work hard to accomplish this end, or you may just focus on keeping your life uncomplicated. People often disappoint you, and if you are in an unhealthy state of mind, you may become fatalistic about life in general.

Wings

The personalities to either side of you on the Enneagram are Eight, the Challenger, and One, the Reformer. A Nine with a stronger Eight-Wing has been labeled "The Referee" by some, and a Nine with a stronger One-Wing has been labeled "The Dreamer." Look at the chapters on these two personalities to decide if you identify more strongly with one of these wings.

Directions of Integration and Disintegration

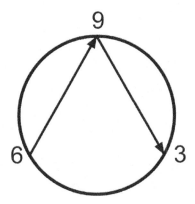

Your direction of integration is toward type Three, the Achiever. When you are emotionally healthy, you exhibit some of the qualities of a healthy Three. You have believed that your own perspective is unimportant, but if you work through this belief, you can see that others value you fully and want to hear your thoughts and feelings. You understand that you hold intrinsic value, and you begin to develop your own interests and talents so you can share them with the world.

If you are less emotionally healthy but still, in secure conditions, you display average Three traits. You may be able to show your value to a few trusted people who are close to you. Under secure circumstances, you deal with stress by being extra productive as a way of trying to prove your worth and impress others.

Your direction of disintegration is towards type Six, the Loyalist. Your first reaction to stressful situations is emotional detachment, but eventually, you may become irritable. Although complaining is typically out of character to you, you may begin vocalizing your displeasure and blaming others. If the stress continues, you become even more anxious and reactive.

Levels of Development

The following is a very brief breakdown of your levels of development as a Nine, so you can begin to recognize your psychological health and warning signs that you may have some work to do.

- **Healthy**
    - **Level 1 (at your best):** You can be present and aware of your own emotions. Your contentment does not depend on the harmony of those around you because you are connected to your inner self. You can form deeper bonds with others.
    - **Level 2:** You are stable and serene. Others are drawn to your accepting nature. Your life is simple and you are genuinely good-natured.
    - **Level 3:** Others seek out your meditation abilities. Your strengths are your optimism, calming influence, and communication skills.

- **Average**
    - **Level 4:** You go along with the desires of others, even when contradictory to your desires. You believe the best in others. Your fear of conflict keeps you from acknowledging your needs.
    - **Level 5:** Because you don't want to be affected by conflict, you disengage from much of life. You walk away from problems and escape into your own thoughts.
    - **Level 6**: You try to keep other people happy by minimizing problems. You feel resigned to the fact that nothing can improve. You are fairly withdrawn and inactive.

- **Unhealthy**
    - **Level 7:** You are emotionally undeveloped and have highly repressed anger. You remove yourself from problems because you feel that you're unable to face them.
    - **Level 8:** You numb yourself to the extent that you may no longer be able to fully function.
    - **Level 9:** You are severely dissociated and unaware of reality. Possible multiple personalities, Schizoid, and Dependent personality disorders.

Subtypes/Instincts

If you are a *social* Nine, you are more active and outgoing than most Nines. You like to participate in community causes and organizations. Even if you are heavily involved in a group, you manage to be unaffected by conflicts within the group, because you are friendly but not deeply involved with others in the group. You keep busy with your participation in a cause, but you are not necessarily internally motivated. You may be easily distracted.

As a *sexual* Nine, you seek someone to share your sense of ease and gentleness. You can be highly sensual and imaginative. The idea of a special union with someone is attractive to you, but you fear to lose your identity because of your inability to express your wants and needs. You may hold back from a relationship and not fully show up emotionally. This can create the tensions that you desperately want to avoid.

Finally, if you are a *self-preservation* Nine, you seek comfort and familiarity above other priorities. You value your alone time and do not appreciate changes to your environment. You may struggle with inactivity and overeating, or you may be very rigid with your diet. Two of your most positive characteristics are your common sense and patience.

Psychological and Spiritual Growth

As a Nine, you value other people more than you value yourself. Take time to reflect on attributes about yourself that are valuable and desirable. Appreciate what you bring to the table.

When you want to complain, try to determine what hidden want or need you have repressed. Would it be so terrible to express this want or need? You may fear criticism and not being taken seriously, so start small with your self-assertion. Practice small assertions until you are comfortable enough to express yourself in something more important, and then keep practicing!

By denying your feelings and devaluing your own opinion, you create disunion within yourself. You will not experience true union with others until you have union within yourself. Asserting yourself is not aggressive; it is positive and will cause others to respect you more.

For many Nines, mindfulness meditation is helpful. Meditation can take many forms, so research effective meditation methods for your type. The most useful meditations for Nines include recognizing and accepting emotions, valuing yourself as much as you value others, and discovering your own intentions and purposes.

Notice physical sensations of discomfort in your body when you encounter conflict. Instead of fleeing, remind yourself that it is naturally occurring and learn to deal with the conflict constructively.

Recognize that some conflicts and pain in the world are unavoidable. You have the gift of mediation, and you can use this gift to genuinely bring more peace to others.

Reflect on a story of growth from fellow Nine. She has become aware that she tends to support other people's plans while sacrificing her own plans. She knows now that it is critical for her to acknowledge her own wants and needs, even when she feels bad for doing so.

This Nine admits that she has trouble getting started with positive action at times because she is often tempted to sit and let life pass her by. She also has trouble concentrating on her own priorities, because she is so used to letting other people's priorities be more important. The habit of letting go of her own desires to "keep the peace" is deeply ingrained in her, and she is used to keeping any anger locked deep inside herself. Sometimes that anger comes exploding out, with damaging effects to herself and others. But now, thanks to learning about herself through teachings from the Enneagram, she is starting to get help.

Through the Enneagram, this woman learned to get help through something called bioenergetic work, which is a type of therapy accomplished through body movement techniques. The body positions held in a bioenergetic session are designed to help participants get in touch with their emotions through physical movement. This particular Nine has discovered her own desires and needs through group sessions in bioenergetics. She has even learned to express her anger safely.

She now feels empowered to pursue her own interests in music, and she finds that her music feels much more authentic thanks to her Enneagram and bioenergetics work. Through a new connection with her true self, she now feels more alive than she has ever felt!

If you are a Nine who is constantly squelching your own needs and wants to keep the peace around you, or if you are keeping anger locked inside yourself, it is our hope that you will continue to learn about your emotions and desires. Find ways to get in touch with them and express them so that you, too, can feel alive and whole.

Relationships

This final section consists of lists with helpful hints *for* Nines in relationships and for people in relationships *with* Nines. These include business relationships, romantic relationships, and parent-child relationships.

Business Relationships FOR *Nines:*
- When speaking to a group, plan what you will say ahead of time and get to the point quickly.
- Stay present and prioritize what needs to be done in each moment.
- Learn to keep to an agenda with deadlines.
- Remember that conflicts are sometimes inevitable; breathe and find constructive ways to deal with conflict.
- Work on making your valuable opinions known.
- Do not be too accommodating to your associates; show that you have a backbone and firmly stand your ground when necessary.

Business Relationships WITH *Nines:*
- Remind them of their personal needs and rights.

- Nines are good at seeing the big picture but need help structuring steps of how to reach the goal. Set short-term objectives for them.
- Ask them for cooperation instead of trying to push them around.
- Be accepting of their personality while challenging them and helping them to take risks.
- Remind them that saying "No" does not always start a conflict.
- Listen to them well and avoid coming on too strong or acting impatient.

Parenting FOR *Nines:*
- You are good at being supportive, kind, and warm. Keep it up!
- Avoid being overly permissive. Accept that you cannot always make your child happy.
- You have to set limits for your child to keep them safe and help them grow into a responsible adult.
- Don't take it personally when your child is upset with you.
- Recognize how you would like your child to behave and remember it's ok to assert these expectations.

Parenting When Your CHILD *Is A Nine*
- Make sure they know you notice and value them.
- Ask how they are feeling during and after conflicts in your home.
- Remind them it is ok to be angry. Help them find healthy outlets for emotions.
- Listen to any concerns they have and do not come across as overly critical.
- Model healthy ways of resolving a conflict.

Romantic Relationships FOR *Nines:*
- Recognize that you have aggression, anxieties, and other feelings you must deal with to have healthy relationships. Get things out in the open instead of suppressing them.
- Express wants and needs clearly.
- Work on staying present and being an active participant in your relationship.
- Find a healthy solo outlet for emotions, like regular exercise.
- Stand up for yourself if you are feeling controlled or ignored.

Romantic Relationships WITH *Nines:*

- Avoid creating pressure, getting impatient, or coming on too strong.
- Know what they need and want by asking them. Give them time to discern the answer.
- Tell them it's ok to say "no," especially if you sense they are reluctant about something.
- Share physical activities, like exercising or cooking together.
- Support them to act when they want to do something.
- Show physical affection. It helps open them up to their feelings.
- Discuss but don't confront.

- Compliment the way they look.
- Share in their enjoyment of life.

Chapter 6: Type 1 – The Reformer

Type 1 Checklist: *Ask yourself if the following statements are true for you.*

- You feel personally obligated to improve yourself and the world.
- You are extremely responsible, sensible, conscientious, and ethical.
- You have a sense of discipline that comes from within.
- You tend to think that nothing is ever quite good enough.
- You are continually aware of flaws in yourself, others, and situations.
- You often feel guilty for being unable to achieve perfection. You also feel guilty for your anger against an imperfect world.
- You follow the rules and expect others to do so as well.
- You are driven and ambitious, sometimes, workaholic.
- You are good at getting things done.
- You are a loyal, responsible, and capable partner and friend.
- You are often tense and have a hard time relaxing.
- You have natural organizational skills.
- You tend to be aware of how your actions might affect future situations.
- You have a deep feeling of purpose for your life and you have a fairly good idea of what that purpose might be.
- You have deep convictions about right and wrong.

If you can relate to more than half of the above statements, you are probably a type One or have a strong One wing. Keep reading to learn more about your type!

Core Belief

The belief that drives your behavior is that you must gain worthiness and love by being as good and perfect as possible. You feel that you need to work diligently towards improving an imperfect world.

Avoidance: *Imperfection*

You avoid making mistakes or appearing wrong at all costs, even though you are acutely aware of your own imperfections and have a strong sense of never being good enough.

Trap: *Making Things Right*

You can get caught up in your attempts to achieve perfection. Your inner criticism and anger at an imperfect world are very damaging to you.

Idealization: *I am good and right.*

This is the image that you wish to project to the world. Although your strong sense of right and wrong aide you in seeking justice, you hold yourself and others to impossible standards in which simple human mistakes are "bad." Your fear is being wrong because this would make you unworthy.

Defense Mechanism: *Reaction Formation*

Reaction formation is a defense mechanism in which any unacceptable emotions are supposedly overcome by an exaggerated display of the exact opposite behavior. You see your anger as a "bad" emotion, so you turn it inward while maintaining an outward appearance of self-control and purposeful action.

Passion: *Anger/Resentment*

As a member of the *Instinctive Triad,* you struggle with anger, even though you view anger as a "bad" emotion. You turn it inwards against yourself; your harsh inner self-critic constantly berates you for your imperfections. Your feelings of having higher standards than everyone else makes you feel irritated and resentful.

Description

You are goal-oriented and concerned with *how* you accomplish your goals. You feel that you must achieve results while still adhering to strict ethical standards. Second-best is unacceptable.

You have most likely felt a strong sense of purpose in your life since childhood. More importantly, you have a good idea of exactly what that purpose might be, and you strive to accomplish that purpose.

Your ethical standards give you strong convictions of social justice. Consequently, you are often committed to causes as a part of your mission to improve the world. Your many positive traits include attention to detail and ability to be objective and fair. You are very principled, valuing integrity, reliable, and responsible. You have a natural talent for organization.

You are used to constantly judging yourself, and your internal dialogue contains phrases such as "I should" and "I must." Unfortunately, you feel that you will never live up to your own standards and you can be deeply unhappy with yourself as a result.

You often do not realize when you appear impatient to others, even though you try to hide and control this emotion. You rarely express anger without thinking it through thoroughly and presenting the offender with a list of past experiences – "proof" that you are right. You have an especially hard time accepting even the most constructive of criticism because you view it as evidence of failure.

Wings

The personalities to either side of you on the Enneagram are Nine, the Peacemaker, and Two, the Helper. A One with a stronger Nine-Wing has been labeled "The Idealist" by some, and a One with a stronger Two-Wing has been labeled "The Advocate." Look at the chapters on these two personalities to decide if you identify more strongly with one of them.

Directions of Integration and Disintegration

Your direction of integration is towards Seven, the Enthusiast. When you are emotionally healthy, you can exhibit some of the qualities of a healthy Seven. As you work through

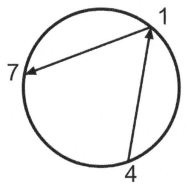

your rigid need for perfection, you become less strict and experience a sense of freedom from obligation. As you accept yourself, you become grateful for the differences of those around you.

If you are less emotionally healthy but still, in secure conditions, you display the traits of an average Seven. This means that you may be less inhibited and express emotions around people you trust. You may allow yourself to express some of your own needs, which may come across as selfish.

Your direction of disintegration is towards Four, the Individualist. If you feel that you have much higher standards than those around you, you become resentful, forcing yourself to do the work that you believe others will not. You become depressed and disillusioned, leading you to isolate and possibly indulge in behaviors that you rigidly kept from allowing yourself before, like eating "forbidden" foods.

Levels of Development

The following is a very brief breakdown of your levels of development as a One, so you recognize your psychological health and warning signs of deterioration:

- **Healthy**
  - **Level 1 (at your best):** You accept the imperfections of yourself and others; you are realistic but still wise and discerning. You strive for truth and justice.
  - **Level 2:** You have strong moral convictions and sense of right and wrong. You try to be mature, rational, and moderate.
  - **Level 3:** You are fair and ethical, valuing integrity and responsibility. You strive for a higher purpose that you sense for yourself.

- **Average**
  - **Level 4:** You are involved in social causes, feeling it is up to you to affect change. You are dissatisfied with the world you live in.
  - **Level 5:** You fear mistakes, making you rigid with feelings and impulses. Possibly workaholic due to obligation.
  - **Level 6:** You are extremely critical of yourself and others. You are often impatient and dissatisfied with other people.

- **Unhealthy**
  - **Level 7:** You are self-righteous and intolerant. Only you know the best way; you judge others severely.
  - **Level 8:** You become obsessive about proclaiming others' imperfections.
  - **Level 9:** You condemn others and try to punish them. You may be severely depressed and/or suicidal. Possibly Obsessive-Compulsive or Depressive personality disorder.

Subtypes/Instincts

If you are a *social* One, you take local and world issues personally and spend your energy attempting to make others care as much as you do. You can't just talk about what's wrong with the world, you need to *do* something about it! You can become so heavily involved in your causes that you cannot develop much of a social life. Although you lack balance in this way, your convictions are admirably strong, and you contribute greatly to the community.

If you are a *sexual* One, you can become a perfectionist about your romantic relationships. Your critical nature makes it difficult to find an acceptable partner, so you get excited when you meet someone who seems to share your values and goals. You may idealize this person and worry that you aren't good enough for them. You may also struggle with being overly critical of your partner. Strengths that you bring to intimate relationships are a strong sense of commitment and devotion to continual growth and improvement.

Finally, if you are a *self-preservation* One, you can be very rigid and even militant about the way you run your household. You have well-formed and firm ideas about nutrition, budgeting, exercise, and maintaining order. You feel that keeping order and cleanliness, along with careful planning, will help ensure your survival somehow. You may become very passionate about preserving your family's health.

Psychological and Spiritual Growth Tips

As a One, you need a sense of balance and compassion to temper your rigid need for perfection, which is unnatural and impossible. Learn to give yourself grace, treat yourself with compassion, and accept yourself as you are. Slowly start to tune out the inner critical voice and allow yourself to relax and take time to do something strictly for enjoyment.

Instead of automatically turning your anger inwards, pause, and question what person, place, or thing you are finding unacceptable. Tell yourself that everything is ok as it is, and mistakes are a natural part of learning and growing. Accept others' imperfections as a part of their beauty and do the same for yourself!

Notice and accept your natural desires and emotions. Instead of dismissing or judging them, observe them and get in the practice of expressing them or writing them down.

You have trouble with physical relaxation, so now learn to allow yourself to feel pleasure while breathing. This may feel uncomfortable at first but take it slow and keep trying. The important part is to relax and inhale slowly, then exhale gently. Do some further research on breathing exercises for tension release.

Perhaps, you can relate to the experience of another One, who felt as if she was being strangled by a compulsion to constantly prove she was worthy. She learned to work hard, put on the façade of being perfect, and not let her feelings show, because she felt that was the only way she could be accepted and loved. Throughout her life, her false ego forced her to different college degrees, careers and anything else possible to escape her fears of being unloved or unacceptable. But she felt that nothing worked, and she was in deep pain.

This One goes on to describe how she was introduced to the Enneagram, and eventually, after a particularly painful rejection, she experienced transformation. She says that she finally learned to lower her defenses and be vulnerable for the first time in her life. She finally realized that she could never be perfect and she needed to rely on a Higher Power to get in touch with her authentic self.

She found serenity by following the blueprints to self-discovery provided by the Enneagram. It was only the beginning of the journey, but by getting started on this journey she found a way to accept and embrace her whole self, even the parts that were less than perfect. By allowing herself to feel helpless, she was able to let go of control and finally trust.

If you are a One who feels stifled and suffocated by the compulsion to be perfect, hopefully, you will also be able to recognize that there is another way. You can be vulnerable and admit your shortcomings. By being human and expressing your fears and emotions, you can learn to trust and feel whole.

Relationships

This section consists of lists with helpful hints *for* Ones in relationships and for people in relationships *with* Ones. These include business relationships, romantic relationships, and parent-child relationships.

Business Relationships FOR *Ones:*
- Use your self-discipline to accomplish your goals but try not to become upset when others aren't trying as hard as you.
- Instead of badgering, try gently encouraging others.
- Look for value in others; appreciate them for their unique qualities.
- Appreciate errors, mistakes, and imperfections as differences.
- Admit mistakes and practice acceptance when you hear constructive criticism.
- Use your sense of ethics to be discerning about right and wrong without judging.
- Point out the positive.

Business Relationships WITH *Ones:*
- Speak respectfully and try not to make them feel foolish.
- Make small gestures like being on time and giving proper instructions.
- Admit errors immediately to clear the air and prevent resentment.
- Notice and compliment specific things like dependability and punctuality.
- Avoid power struggles and work cooperatively.
- Demonstrate how two "right" ways can co-exist.
- Avoid making agreements that you cannot keep.
- Ask them to be direct with anger.
- Use their ideas to help you see how things can be improved.
- Remind them to share responsibility with others.

Parenting FOR *Ones:*
- You are good at teaching responsibility and moral values. Keep it up!
- Allow silliness and expression of a wide range of emotions.
- If you must discipline firmly, do it with love and be sure your child knows they are forgiven. Explain that they need to be held accountable.
- Remember they are children, and they will be messy and imperfect. Embrace their beautiful imperfections.
- Be gentle and clear when expressing expectations.

Parenting When Your CHILD *Is A One*
- Model acceptance of imperfections and admit your own mistakes.
- Give grace freely, because they likely are harshly criticizing themselves on the inside.
- Praise responsibility and conscientious behavior.

- Affirm that it's ok to make mistakes and ask for help.
- Check in with their emotions. Ask if they are angry when they make mistakes and give time and space to express that anger.
- Encourage them to try new things, even if they fear failure.

Romantic Relationships FOR *Ones:*
- Appreciate differences between you and your partner.
- Express worries but try to laugh at yourself when you get uptight.
- Tolerate and enjoy your partner's point of view.
- Practice forgiveness toward yourself and your partner.
- Talk openly about any anger you may be feeling toward yourself.
- Give yourself an outlet to release tension and frustration you may be feeling toward the other person.

Romantic Relationships WITH *Ones:*
- Bring fun activities and laughter to your relationship.
- Help them be less critical of themselves and accepting of their mistakes.
- Remind them to share their frustrations.
- Take your share of responsibilities so that they don't do all the work.
- Reassure them that they are valued the way they are.
- Compliment achievements.
- Tell them you value their advice.
- Apologize if you have been inconsiderate and model admitting your mistakes with ease.

The Feeling Triad (Types 2, 3 & 4)

Chapter 7: Type 2 – The Helper

Type 2 Checklist: *Ask yourself if the following statements are true for you.*

- You care deeply about other people and the details of their lives.
- You feel best about yourself when you are meaningfully engaged with others.
- You genuinely enjoy supporting other people with attention and care.
- You are especially good at remembering important details about other people.
- You try to do nice things so others will think well of you.
- You have had trouble with not taking enough care of yourself.
- Sometimes, people have accused you of having "boundary issues" or being a "people-pleaser."
- You sometimes struggle to find self-worth outside of your relationships.
- You are very sensitive to and perceptive about others' feelings
- You have a good sense of humor, and you are fun-loving.
- You can become upset when others don't sense your needs as well as you sense their needs.
- You genuinely enjoy seeing the best in others.
- You fear rejection because it makes you feel worthless.
- You are drawn toward jobs that revolve around helping people.
- You tend to be generous and considerate.

If you can relate to more than half of the above statements, you're probably a Two or you have a strong Two wing. Keep reading to learn more about your type!

Core Belief

The belief that drives your behavior is that you must give fully to others to be loved. At your core, you believe that you are only worthwhile and loveable because you are loving and needed.

Avoidance: *Your Own Needs*

You would rather help others and meet their needs than focus on your own wants and needs because you believe that doing so would make you appear needy. As a result, you deny and avoid any personal needs that you may have.

Trap: *Being of Service*

There is potential for you to be so caught up in your obsession with being of service that you thoroughly exhaust yourself. You can be extremely busy with all your commitments, but when someone new asks for help, you still say yes.

Idealization: *I am helpful.*

This is the image that you try to project to the world because you believe it is what makes you worthwhile. You fear that if you were not able to help others, you would be seen negatively in the eyes of others and ultimately be rejected.

Defense Mechanism: *Repression*

Repression is keeping some feeling out of conscious awareness. For you, repression keeps your own needs out of the picture. You have an incredible ability to sense and fulfill the needs of others, but you use this to avoid being present and aware of your own needs.

Passion: *Pride*

You run the risk of thinking that you, and you alone, can help and/or save certain people. When pride is active in you, you are trying to be appreciated and loved by appearing selfless and giving.

Description

You are the kind of person who remembers everyone's birthday, stays up late to take care of someone or drives across town to deliver food to a sick friend. You are warm and emotional, and you devote much energy to personal relationships. People appreciate that you notice and think of "the little things."

You may excel in a profession that involves helping others, like teaching or nursing. You know how to make a home comfortable and inviting. If you have a family, you are absolutely in your element when caring for a sick child or spouse. Not all Twos are in a helping profession or have a family to take care of, though. You may not even recognize the extent of your involvement in assisting others.

As selfless as you appear on the outside, you thrive on feeling helpful and needed, so your self-sacrifice is not without ulterior motives. Being needed makes you feel important and being helpful makes you feel virtuous. Reading this may be a surprise to you, because you may have thoroughly convinced yourself of your own selflessness.

You may remember times when you became resentful because someone didn't thank you or show appreciation for your assistance. You may feel entitled to some thanks; after all, you worked hard and deserve some gratitude.

Because you spend so much time and energy helping others, you often forget to take care of yourself. Or you may feel that you don't really have many needs. Or when asked, you may not even know what you want and need! This is not uncommon for Twos. However, you do have wants and needs of your own, and if you don't take the time to attend to them you can get utterly burned out.

Friends or family members might say that you are a "people-pleaser." This means that you try to get people to like you by doing things for them. The reason for this isn't that you are selfish. It's because deep down, you feel that you have no worth of your own unless you are helpful and needed.

Wings

The personalities to either side of you on the Enneagram are One, the Reformer, and Three, the Achiever. A Two with a stronger One-Wing has been labeled "The Servant" by some, and a Two with a stronger Three-Wing has been labeled "The Host/Hostess." Look at the chapters on these two personalities to decide if you identify more strongly with one of these.

Directions of Integration and Disintegration

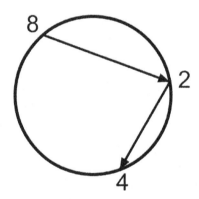

Your direction of integration is toward type Four, the Individualist. This means that when you are emotionally healthy, you exhibit some qualities of a healthy Four. As you become willing to express your needs and hidden emotions, you learn to accept yourself. You find that you can support others in a healthy way, without trying to get them to like you. You also begin to be able to accept your own humanity and so you achieve more intimacy with others in healthy relationships.

If you are less emotionally healthy but still, in secure conditions, you display the traits of an average Four. When you are feeling sure of yourself, you may be able to admit your needs and feelings to a few people that you are comfortable with. Since this is rare for you, you might become moody, selfish, and over-sensitive at these times.

Your disintegration is towards Eight, the Challenger. You feel stressed when you feel that your helpfulness is not noticed or appreciated, and this is when disintegration happens. You display characteristics of average to unhealthy Eights, meaning that you act out in bossy and controlling ways to make people notice you. At particularly bad times, you might even become extremely confrontational and angry.

Levels of Development

The following is a very brief breakdown of your levels of development as a Two, so you can begin to recognize your psychological health and warning signs that of emotional deterioration.

- **Healthy**
  - **Level 1 (at your best):** You realize you're allowed to take care of yourself. You love and are loved unconditionally. You believe good things can happen without your help. You are humble and charitable.
  - **Level 2:** You are thoughtful, warm-hearted, and sincere in compassion. You are genuinely concerned about others' needs.
  - **Level 3:** You value service but also take care of yourself. You generously encourage, love, and nurture others.

- **Average**
  - **Level 4:** "People pleasing" starts. You have good intentions on the surface; underneath, you want to be liked. You can resort to the flattery of others.
  - **Level 5:** You feel a strong desire to be needed; manipulate others to make them depend on you. You are prideful as you remind others of how caring you are. Can be intrusive in your "helpfulness."
  - **Level 6:** You feel others take you for granted and owe you recognition. You try to instill guilt in others for not caring about your needs.

- **Unhealthy**
  - **Level 7:** You project the image of having done nothing wrong while manipulating others into feeling sympathy. You deceive yourself about your motives, believing you are unselfish.
  - **Level 8:** You are controlling and feel entitled to receive repayment for all you have done. You coerce others to give you what they owe.
  - **Level 9:** You feel victimized, so you rationalize any manipulative behavior. Possible Histrionic Personality Disorder or Factitious Disorder.

Subtypes/Instincts

If you are a *social* Two, you wish to be friends with as many people as possible. You make yourself indispensable to any group that you are in by becoming intricately involved in the lives of its members. You offer a sympathetic listening ear to anyone in a crisis, you dispense advice, and offer support to as many people as possible. You like helping important people. You are probably very outgoing and excellent at remembering other people's names. You may struggle with becoming over-committed due to your inability to say "no."

If you are a *sexual* Two, you crave to be as close as possible with your partner. You find out about their preferences, wants, needs, and hobbies, and then do everything you can to provide those things to them. You focus much of your sole attention and affection on a mate, making them want to spend more time with you. You are often the initiator of physical touch. If you are psychologically unhealthy, you may become obsessed with a significant other and not be able to let go of them.

Finally, as *self-preservation* Two, you nurture and take care of those around you to fulfill your need for love and satisfaction with yourself. You hope others will return the favor by taking care of you, but you don't know how to ask for what you want or need. All you can do is drop hints and keep hoping, but sometimes, the others never reciprocate. Because your own needs are not met, you may overindulge in food, alcohol, or other addictive substances because on some level, you feel you "deserve" to indulge. This is dangerous, but you may not know how else to deal with your feelings of loneliness and rejection.

Psychological and Spiritual Growth

Your growth as a Two depends on your recognition that you can care for yourself and others at the same time. In fact, if you really wish to be helpful and nurturing to others, you absolutely *must* care for your own spiritual and physical needs first. Only then will you be in the best possible condition to attend to the needs of those around you.

Similarly, you only reach the emotional intimacy that you crave with others by first recognizing and expressing your own emotions. As a member of the *Feeling Triad*, your emotional issues center around shame. You are ashamed of your own needs and unpleasant emotions, but you need to become comfortable with the fact that it is normal and healthy to have unpleasant emotions and to have needs of your own.

This change cannot happen overnight, of course. Start by reflecting on how you are truly feeling and what needs are not being met. As you begin to be able to recognize your emotions and needs, try voicing them to someone you trust and are very close to. As you learn that you will not be rejected for expressing yourself, you will realize that your worth does not come from denying your needs or constantly being useful to others; it comes from within you.

If you are over-committed, realize that it would be so much more beneficial for everyone if you were to focus on one or two causes or groups that you feel most passionate about. You'll have more time to care for yourself and be healthier as a result. A healthier, more grounded you can give to those you care about with more energy and love.

Consider the experience of a Two who, after experiencing self-discovery through the Enneagram, began to reflect on former past relationships. He realized that he had arrogantly felt that his significant others and close friends truly needed his advice, love, help, and wisdom. Although he was not meaning to be manipulative and he felt that he was being sincere, he began to realize that he was using these other people to meet his own needs.

This Two states that he gravitated towards others whom he thought he could help by being understanding and helping others to understand them. He wanted to be the one and only person who could meet another person's needs. He found his self-worth in being needed and felt panic and desperation when he felt that someone no longer needed him. He would even take great measures to become what he thought someone needed him to be.

Unfortunately, these intense relationships often took a nasty turn when this Two realized that he was being controlled and manipulated. He would feel trapped in the role that he had created for himself, and then he would want to be free.

Finally, after acquiring self-knowledge through the Enneagram and undergoing years of therapy, he now realizes that he had deep rage, loneliness, and sadness inside himself. He now feels able to express his own needs without feeling at risk of being abandoned. He knows that by meeting his own needs he is lifting a burden off of other people (the burden he placed on them by trying to meet his needs through helping them). He feels that he now is moving closer to becoming his authentic self.

If any of that Two's struggles sound like your own, now you know that you are not alone and you can find freedom! Expressing your needs and caring for yourself do *not* make you more likely to be abandoned. In fact, self-care will make you a more genuine and grounded version of yourself, and people will be even more drawn to you than before.

Relationships

This section consists of lists with helpful hints *for* Twos in relationships and for people in relationships *with* Twos. These include business relationships, romantic relationships, and parent-child relationships.

Business Relationships FOR *Twos:*
- Recognize when you are overdoing things or becoming too intrusive/involved and step back.
- Try doing something the way *you* want to do it but have been too ashamed or fearful to suggest.
- Instead of jumping in and offering to help, wait to be asked sometimes.
- Try helping because you *want* to help, not because you are seeking approval.
- Take time to fulfill your needs.
- Practice saying no.
- Tell truths honestly without a positive spin.

Business Relationships WITH *Twos:*
- Be gentle with criticism.

- Tell them that you appreciate their contributions; be specific.
- In conflicts, ask them to take responsibility for getting what they want rather than indirectly blaming others.
- Connect with them in valuing partnership, personal contact, and warmth.
- Don't assume that they will be the one to help when a volunteer is needed. Ask others to help before coming to them.
- Help them set boundaries with anyone that takes advantage of them.
- Help them take time out for themselves.

Parenting FOR *Twos:*
- You are good at listening, encouraging, and loving unconditionally. Keep it up!
- Keep having fun and being playful with your children.
- Don't second-guess everything you do. Everyone makes mistakes in parenting and most mistakes are not detrimental.
- Your protective nature can be a good thing, but let your children try new things, face fears, and make mistakes.
- Don't be hurt when your children do not remember to thank you.
- Resist the urge to guilt-trip your children.

Parenting When Your CHILD *Is A Two:*
- Model expressing your needs and feelings politely.
- Give criticism gently and in the form of suggestion.
- Show appreciation for the help that they give and be specific.
- Give attention to them generously, so they don't feel the need to act a certain way to get your attention.
- Encourage them to talk about their feelings and to spend time alone doing something they enjoy.

Romantic Relationships FOR Twos*:*
- Choose relationships where your authentic self is appreciated and celebrated.
- Pay attention to your own needs instead of constantly immersing yourself in the other person's needs.
- Spend time alone doing something healthy that meets your needs.
- Practice expressing your needs and wants.
- Don't manipulate with guilt if you feel unappreciated. Instead, ask yourself what need you have that hasn't been met.
- Don't do things for the other person to get more love—just do them because you love them.

Romantic Relationships WITH *Twos:*
- Reassure them that they are interesting to you and that you love them.
- Be gentle with any criticism.
- Share plenty of fun times.
- Take an interest in their problems; don't take advantage of their nature by letting them constantly focus on your problems.

- Let them know they are special to you.
- Tell them you're glad to be seen with them.
- Encourage them to take time for themselves.
- Ask them what they need and how they are feeling.

Chapter 8: Type 3 – The Achiever

Type 3 Checklist: *Ask yourself if the following statements are true for you.*

- You want to be the best at everything you do.
- You are willing to do whatever it takes to stand out as the best.
- You are goal-oriented.
- You have trouble understanding people who are not as motivated as you to pursue dreams.
- You have learned to adapt easily to achieve your goals.
- You value efficiency and effectiveness.
- You tend to brush aside your own feelings to get things done.
- You often push yourself too hard.
- When you are struggling, you try to convince others that you are fine.
- As a child, you learned to perform in ways that would earn praise and positive attention.
- It is important to you that you appear successful to others.
- You are very competitive and love winning.
- You are good at appearing confident and optimistic, even when you do not feel that way.
- You can become short-tempered when you face the possibility of failure.

If you can relate to more than half of the above statements, you probably are a Three or you have a strong Three wing. Keep reading to learn more about your type!

Core Belief

The belief that drives your behavior is the world values winners, and you must achieve success to be worthwhile and loved. You believe that worth comes from doing, not simply being.

Avoidance: *Failure*

You have a deep fear of failure because success is worthless in your eyes. You avoid sitting around "doing nothing" because that is almost the equivalent of failure to you. If you were ever unable to accomplish anything, you feel that you would have no value.

Trap: *Achieving (Efficiency)*

You can be so caught up in your goal of doing everything as well as possible and as quickly as possible that the goal controls you. You can become so alienated from yourself that you don't know what your desires, feelings, or interests are.

Idealization: *I am successful/I am a winner.*

You wish to present an image of success in the world. You thrive on the approval and applause that you get from this image, and you find your identity and self-worth in achievement.

Defense Mechanism: *Identification*

Identification is a defense mechanism in which you unconsciously take characteristics of another person into your own personality and sense of self. When you feel threatened by perceived or possibly real failure, you tend to identify with someone that you admire and see as successful. In doing this, you avoid failure and maintain a self-image of success.

Passion: *Vanity (Deceit)*

You hide any inner qualities that you feel are inadequate and strive to only display qualities that you believe a "winner" has. Your passion of vanity or deceit starts with you deceiving yourself about who you are. Your self-deception might eventually run so deep that you are able to deceive those around you easily and without remorse.

Description

Your type has been called The Initiator, Succeeder, Performer, Achiever, and Motivator. You are decisive, risk-taking, adaptable, and optimistic. Your energy and motivation are usually much greater than the others. You expect success from yourself, and you usually get it.

You are good at juggling multiple commitments at a time and you rarely relax. Even when you are enjoying hobbies or spending time with friends, you are usually looking for recognition for being successful. You feel you may not have value outside of your achievements. You fear failure because your image and self-worth are wrapped up in what you *do* and not who you *are*.

Some of your best qualities are your ability to take initiative and get things done. You are adaptable and good at figuring out what others expect of you, and then meeting those expectations. At your best, you can achieve great things and inspire greatness in others.

Underneath your image of achievement is a tendency to brush aside your feelings and pretend everything is fine, even if you are suffering from extreme anxiety or depression. You feel enormous pressure to be outstanding, and you fear to stop to rest might lead you to failure.

As a member of the *Feeling Triad*, you struggle with shame. Your shame is centered around any inner qualities that you think are inadequate, and you deal with it by identifying with people that you see as successful.

Wings

The personalities to either side of you on the Enneagram are Two, the Helper, and Four, the Individualist. A Three with a Two-Wing has been labeled "The Charmer" by some, and a Three with a Four-Wing has been labeled "The Professional." Read the chapters on these two personalities to decide if you identify more strongly with one of them.

Directions of Integration and Disintegration

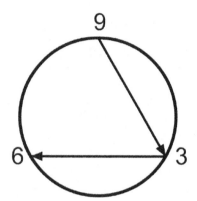

Your integration is toward type Six, the Loyalist. This means that when you are emotionally healthy, you exhibit qualities of a healthy Six. When you let go of your fears of failure, you are less competitive and cooperate with others. You find value from sharing goals and offering support. You may learn to ask for help for yourself and to trust others. In this reliance on others, you can become more selfless and act like a leader.

If you are less emotionally healthy but still secure, you display traits of average Sixes. When you are feeling sure of yourself, you can admit your anxieties to a few trusted people. For example, you may be able to maintain your image of achievement all day at the office, but you come home in the evening and unload your issues to a sympathetic partner.

Your disintegration is towards Nine, the Peacemaker. When you are under too much pressure for too long, you may start to just "go through the motions" to get through the day. You still maintain the appearance of accomplishing things for a while, but as stress continues, you might just shut down and withdraw from people.

Levels of Development

The following is a very brief breakdown of your levels of development as a Two, so you can begin to recognize your psychological health and warning signs of deterioration.

- **Healthy**
  - **Level 1 (at your best):** You let go of dependency on applause and believe in your intrinsic value. Working cooperatively with others is your authentic self.
  - **Level 2:** You are self-assured and energetic. Others are drawn to your charm and grace.
  - **Level 3:** You strive to be your best and inspire others.

- **Average**
  - **Level 4:** You are driven to be the best. You worry about performing well and fear failure. You compare yourself to others.
  - **Level 5:** You worry about how others see you; you hide your inner qualities under attributes you believe will make you look successful.
  - **Level 6:** You feel jealous of others and their success, but on the outside, you appear arrogant. You try to impress others.

- **Unhealthy**
  - **Level 7:** You fear humiliation and are willing to be unethical to maintain your image of success.
  - **Level 8:** You are immoral in your attempts to hide your mistakes. You are very jealous of others and willing to hurt them in order to win.
  - **Level 9:** You lose touch with reality and attempt to sabotage others. You obsessively hide or destroy any evidence of failures. Possible Narcissistic Personality Disorder.

Subtypes/Instincts

If you are a *social* Three, you seek tangible recognition so others may see your achievements. You adapt into any environment so you can avoid humiliation and be accepted everywhere. Because you are such a chameleon, you may lose track of your goals and become less of an achiever. You may be distracted by the need to impress your peers and stop pursuing tangible successes.

If you are a *sexual* Three, you aim to be as desirable as possible. Potential mates may see you as very charming and attractive, but your insecurities might keep you from being intimate with anyone. You wish to be appreciated for your inner qualities, but you fear to reveal these qualities because others may reject you.

Finally, as a *self-preservation* Three, you may be a "workaholic." You find worth in your ability to provide for yourself or your family. You are so driven by this priority that you cannot slow down or take time off. This addiction to work affects personal relationships and your physical health. Your family and/or significant others may not understand that you show love by working hard to provide for them.

Psychological and Spiritual Growth

As a Three, you can grow by realizing that your feelings and inner qualities do not have to be separate from your success and value. If you can get in touch with your emotions, you will find that you are able to function better as a whole human being. Thus, you find satisfaction in your work and relationships instead of wrapping your self-worth up in achievement.

Try slowing your pace and notice what happens to you internally and externally. Welcome feelings as normal parts of being human. Try to listen to someone without agenda. Instead of obeying the urge to self-promote or look good, tune in to what someone else is saying and try not to interrupt.
Your fear of failure cripples your intrinsic self-worth, so you pay more attention to people who are "winners." Try finding value in all people and realizing that they are much more than the image that they present to the public. Then, try that strategy on yourself. Exercise compassion and self-forgiveness when you feel you have failed and remember that making mistakes is part of being human. Failures are opportunities for growth.

Finally, remind yourself that everything is not dependent on your efforts. When you stop racing around to pursue achievement, you are present in the moment and there for your loved ones. Speaking of loved ones, remind yourself that they value you for who you *are*, not for what you *do!*

One Three shared that, after learning from the Enneagram, she learned to seek less approval from the outside world and stop finding worth in achievement. Before, she had believed in the core that she needed to be seen as successful. She would take any unsettling emotions and use them to fuel some sort of productivity, but this would cut off her ability to be in touch with those emotions. She felt like people would abandon her if she made a mistake.

Now that she has worked on herself through Enneagram teachings and therapy, this Three says that she needs less approval from others. She can admit when she makes a mistake without trying to cover up the truth. She can be honest with herself about her inner emotions and deal with them more effectively as they come up.

She says that she now feels like she is able to work more cooperatively with people and she is able to prioritize people over accomplishments. Her relationships have more meaning now, and she is able to make true friends more than she could before.
If you feel that your sense of acceptance and approval come from your achievements and you are terrified of failure, you're not alone! You can find help and healing by becoming vulnerable and recognizing your emotions, no matter how unsettling they are.

Relationships

This final section consists of lists with helpful hints *for* Threes in relationships and for people in relationships *with* Threes. These include business relationships, romantic relationships, and parent-child relationships.

Business Relationships FOR *Threes:*
- Work on developing patience for others who do not work as quickly as you.
- Slow your pace and devote yourself to the process.
- Admit mistakes and find opportunities for growth from them.
- Work with others instead of competing.
- Find ways to make your everyday duties creative.
- Listen to others when in a meeting and take a back seat.

Business Relationships WITH *Threes:*
- Let them know you appreciate their work.
- Speed up in talking to them.
- Avoid getting in the way of their progress or taking too much of their time.
- Join them in being active and getting results.
- When conflicts arise, let them vent if they are staying on task.
- Remind them people are more important than achievement.
- Remind them success can come from many different styles.
- Give honest but not overly judgmental feedback.

Parenting FOR *Threes:*
- You are good at being consistent, dependable, and loyal. Keep it up!
- Don't cut your time with your children short so that you can work more.
- It's ok to expect your children to be responsible but don't be too rigid.
- Don't punish them harshly for mistakes.
- Allow them to explore different activities without expecting a particular result.

Parenting When Your CHILD *Is A Three*
- Tell them you are proud of their accomplishments.
- Show appreciation for traits that have nothing to do with accomplishment—like generosity, honesty, and fairness.
- Foster an environment of peace and harmony at home.
- Tell them you enjoy being around them.
- Encourage them to try new things that do not have to become a competition.
- Model expressing feelings, doubts, and admitting mistakes at home.

Romantic Relationships FOR *Threes:*
- Remind yourself that your partner loves you for who you *are*, not what you *do*.
- Learn to develop empathy and understanding for yourself and your significant other.
- Practice telling them when experiencing doubts or anxieties.

- Be truthful about real feelings.
- Genuinely listen to them, without letting your mind race about what you should be accomplishing.
- Enjoy simple activities together, like taking walks.
- Let them decide what you do together sometimes.

Romantic Relationships WITH *Threes:*
- Treat them with love and compassion when they feel that they have failed.
- Encourage them to take time to "smell the roses," pay attention to feelings, and really listen to you.
- Show and tell them what is important to you.
- Tell them that you like being around them.
- Tell them when you're proud of them or their accomplishments.
- Give them honest feedback, without being overly judgmental.
- Encourage them to slow down and pay attention to their well-being.
- Tell them you value them for who they are.

Chapter 9: Type 4 – The Individualist

Type 4 Checklist: *Ask yourself if the following statements are true for you.*

- You are in touch with your emotions and listen to what they are telling you.
- At times, you are deeply in touch with human nature.
- You like to creatively express yourself.
- You can become quite self-absorbed.
- You are comfortable telling others how you feel.
- You thrive on being an individual, but sometimes, you wish you weren't so different from others.
- You care about beauty and personal taste.
- You feel alone and misunderstood.
- People have accused you of being over-dramatic and too sensitive.
- You find ways to be unique, no matter what you are doing.
- Sometimes, you feel very empty and depressed.
- You feel that there is something out there that would make you feel more whole and complete.
- You tend to compare yourself to others and are envious when you feel they have something you are missing in life.
- You have trouble planning things in advance.
- You admire what is beautiful, truthful, and noble in life.

If you can relate to more than half of the above statements, you are likely a Four or have a strong Four wing. Keep reading to learn more about your type!

Core Belief

The belief driving your behavior is that something important is missing in your life, and you must find it. You feel that your purpose is to express your authentic self and create beauty and meaning in life.

Avoidance: *Being Ordinary*

You fear and avoid what you view as common and insignificant in life because you feel these things have no worth. Deep down, you are afraid that you are missing the things that would make you truly unique, so you conceal what you think is ordinary.

Trap: *Being Unique*

You can be so ensnared by your goal of being different that you continually focus on what is missing in your life. As a result, you are unable to see and appreciate who you really are or what is good in your world.

Idealization: *I am authentic.*

You strive to distinguish yourself from others by emphasizing everything that is different about you. You find your value in this self-image.

Defense Mechanism: *Introjection*

Through introjection, you pick up traits that you view as unique and special to set yourself apart. This helps you avoid and overcome the ordinariness that you fear. You also internalize blame when things go wrong. This reinforces your feelings of loneliness and being misunderstood.

Passion: *Envy*

You incessantly compare yourself to others, both consciously and unconsciously. You feel something is missing from your life and you envy those who seem to have this "something." You feel you are somehow unlucky or that you have suffered more than others, and you have trouble feeling good about yourself.

Description

You maintain your identity by seeing yourself as different from others on a fundamental level. Your sense of individuality comes from being unique and special, but also from feeling that something important is missing from your life.

Some of your strengths are your abilities to experience feelings on a deep level and find meaning in life. You are very expressive, and you often can describe feelings and experiences in a very eloquent way. Your emotional honesty inspires others to get in touch with their own inner experiences and emotions. You can be very empathetic, supportive, passionate, and witty. You easily form bonds with other people, and you can be an excellent listener.

At times, you become completely preoccupied with your emotions and drift away into your thoughts and memories. You need to be different makes you feel alone and misunderstood. You feel that "something" is missing, although you may not be able to define what that "something" is. You long for someone to come into your life and appreciate you for all your uniqueness.

You often suffer from low self-esteem. As a member of the *Feeling Triad*, you struggle with shame centered around your identity. You avoid this shame by focusing on your uniqueness.

You might have created a fantasy self – an imagined self-image with the individuality and special qualities you think you are missing. You try to project the image of this fantasy self, but you feel depressed about who you really are. Sometimes you imagine that others have much worse opinions of you than they do, and you can become extremely sensitive to how they treat you. You hold on to resentments towards people who have hurt you in the past.

Directions of Integration and Disintegration

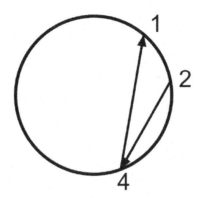

Your integration is towards type One, the Reformer. When you are emotionally healthy, you look like a healthy One. You start to notice how preoccupied you have been with your "unique disadvantages" and realize this is unhealthy. You see yourself more realistically and gain acceptance of your true self. You become practical and grounded, and you have a desire to help with worthwhile pursuits to benefit others.

If you are less healthy but still secure, you display the traits of average Ones, becoming more impatient and critical of other people than you usually are. Instead of silently comparing yourself to others, you begin to focus on their faults and become irritable. You may want to stay constantly busy and work towards improvement without stopping.

Your disintegration is towards type Two, the Helper. When emotionally wounded, you first withdraw from people. Once you realize that you are probably driving people away, you try "people pleasing" for a while, trying to make people need you by being constantly helpful. If this phase of discontent and emotional manipulation lasts, you become clingy and possessive of your loved ones.

Levels of Development

The following is a very brief breakdown of your levels of development as a Two, so you can begin to recognize your psychological health and warning signs of emotional deterioration.

- **Healthy**
    - **Level 1 (at your best):** You let go of your belief that you are missing something and your projected uniqueness. Your creativity is inspirational to others.
    - **Level 2:** You strive to have a meaningful identity based on your inner, true self. You are aware of your feelings and intuitive to others.
    - **Level 3:** You are emotionally honest and strong, can express vulnerability, and remain true to yourself. You relate to others authentically.

- **Average**
  - **Level 4:** You work prolong emotions and promote an image of "the special one." You are dramatic and can withdraw into imagination.
  - **Level 5:** You manipulate others into treating you with special care. You struggle with envy if people around you are happy.
  - **Level 6**: You feel sorry for yourself and treating others as if they have no value. You believe you don't need to conform to the rules that apply to everyone else. You escape into a fantasy world.

- **Unhealthy**
  - **Level 7:** You resent life because of all the disappointments you have suffered. You reject anyone that does not support your emotional demands. You loathe yourself and are too fatigued to function.
  - **Level 8:** You hate yourself to the point of delusion and feel tormented by life. You blame yourself and everyone else, and you refuse to accept help.
  - **Level 9:** You reach despair and self-destruction. You may abuse addictive substances and are at risk of suicidal tendencies. Possible Avoidant, Depressive, or Narcissistic personality disorders.

Subtypes/Instincts

If you are a *social* Four, you want desperately to belong to a social crowd but fear that you don't fit in. You create a false image that is less restrained than you feel; even though you know this is a lie, you use it to feel like you belong. You express your individuality through your own personal style, but you are also trying to hide your insecurities and shame. When stressed, you withdraw from social contact almost completely for a time.

If you are a *sexual* Four, you have the potential for great intimacy in relationships. You may become quickly infatuated or possessive of a significant other. You believe you will feel complete by finding that "missing something" in the right person and place high expectations on your romantic partners. When these expectations are unmet, you become resentful, switching from feeling love to hate at a moment's notice. Your emotional nature can be both attractive and off-putting to others.

Finally, as a *self-preservation* Four, you look for fulfillment in luxury and comfort. Your envy fuels your need for expensive things, and you may indulge yourself in special luxuries when you are dealing with emotional pain. This may go to the extreme of addictive substances or behaviors when you feel your environment is not meeting your emotional needs.

Recommendations for Psychological and Spiritual Growth

As a Four, you grow by learning to move beyond the pain of your past and appreciating and accepting the present moment. Though you have been hurt or disappointed, you are not lacking anything as a human being. If you begin practice focusing on gratitude for what you have instead of mourning what you feel is missing, you find satisfaction and accept that wholeness exists right now, in the present moment.

Your value comes from being yourself, not from setting yourself apart. Try appreciating the "ordinary" traits in yourself and in others. You may even benefit from writing down commonplace things and characteristics that you appreciate as you go about your daily life.

You often experience very intense emotions that can be confusing or even debilitating. Remind yourself that feelings aren't facts, and feelings change all the time. Maintain a steady course of action even when you are experiencing intense feelings. Acknowledge and accept your feelings while refusing to be dominated by them.

You have been expecting others to focus on you. When you find yourself monopolizing conversational focus, gently redirect the attention back to other people. You may have to do this often, but it will get easier with practice. Build up others in your conversations and see how much joy you feel by making them happy. By cultivating happiness in others, you can start to overcome your envy and longing for that mysterious "something" that is missing.

One particular type Four says he is now discovering how to deal with his reckless behavior tendencies after learning from the Enneagram. He says that he often engages in risky behavior after enough emotional pressure has built up inside him. He behaves recklessly because he feels that he has to do something, anything, to break free from the feeling of pressure inside.
After studying the Enneagram, this Four is now more aware of the times when tension builds up inside him. Often, when he feels the urge to do something reckless, he talks to someone who is more rational than himself. If they are shocked at what he wants to do, he realizes that he is being irrational and that he needs to reflect on the emotions inside him that are making him feel that way. In this way, he is able to balance his extreme tendencies and he is becoming more in touch with himself.

Perhaps you, too, tend to act irrationally when you feel too much pressure inside you. Please understand that this tendency can be damaging to yourself and the people around you. You can unlearn this behavior by being willing to explore your feelings without letting them dominate you!

Relationships

This section consists of lists with helpful hints *for* Fours in relationships and for people in relationships *with* Fours. These include business relationships, romantic relationships, and parent-child relationships.

Business Relationships FOR *Fours:*
- You have been self-conscious in front of groups. Take on a role that will put you in front of people so you can practice and grow more comfortable.

- Stay connected with people by asking them about the details of their lives and complimenting their ideas.
- Plan to stay productive even when experiencing intense emotions.
- Appreciate the small, ordinary things that other people do at the workplace.
- When you feel criticized, pause instead of reacting. Try to learn and grow from this experience.
- Keep a list of your positive qualities in a place that you can access it easily when you are filled with self-doubt.

Business Relationships WITH *Fours:*
- Appreciate their emotional sensitivity and creativity.
- Avoid insisting they "calm down" or telling them they're overreacting.
- Join them in valuing individualism.
- In conflict, challenge them to stick to middle ground instead of withdrawing or having an angry outburst.
- Not taking what they say when they are angry or upset literary is advised since it might just be a temporary feeling.
- Encourage them to express their thoughts safely and directly instead of falling into a pit of depression.
- Compliment them when they do something well.

Parenting FOR *Fours:*
- You're good at supporting creativity and originality. Keep it up!
- You have a natural ability to get in touch with your feelings, so help your child learn how to do this too.
- Don't escape into your head or become too self-absorbed; remain present for your child.
- Don't be too critical.
- Watch your level of protectiveness. Some are good; too much can be damaging.

Parenting When Your CHILD *Is A Four*
- Be careful with criticism, as they are very sensitive.
- Encourage their imagination through artistic or other pursuits.
- Tell them you enjoy spending time with them.
- Encourage them to be grateful for ordinary things.
- Ask them to tell you about their feelings.
- Remind them that you love them just as they are and they don't need anything else to be worthy of your love.

Romantic Relationships FOR *Fours:*
- Focus on all the positive things about your partner and your relationship, even the small "ordinary" things.
- When you feel overwhelmed by emotions, don't unleash them all at once on your unsuspecting partner. Take deep breaths and try to explain it logically.

- Focus on your significant other in conversation at least as often as you focus on yourself.
- Remind yourself that your feelings aren't the only reality.
- Resist the urge to "punish" your partner when you feel neglected.
- Don't expect your partner to complete you. You are two individuals who enjoy each other's company and enhance each other's lives.

Romantic Relationships WITH *Fours:*
- Expect mood shifts that are unrelated to what you do or don't do.
- Try to remain steady, calm, and reliable under pressure.
- Set boundaries about your availability; don't succumb to attempts to monopolize your time.
- Give space in times of moodiness.
- Encourage them to slowly take in genuine compliments and bring these compliments to their attention if they don't notice them.
- Expect them to pursue you when you are distant and push you away when you are available.
- Don't tell them they are too sensitive or overreacting.
- Help them learn to love and value themselves.
- Appreciate their gifts of insight and empathy.
- Help them fight their inner critic and support them as they learn to express their feelings directly.

The Thinking Triad
(Types 5, 6, & 7)

Chapter 10: Type 5 – The Investigator

Type 5 Checklist: *Ask yourself if the following statements are true for you.*

- You can be highly innovative and inventive.
- You look beneath the surface of things to arrive at deep insights.
- You are independent and may be labeled as a "loner" or "misfit."
- You are happy to pursue your interests and curiosity wherever they take you.
- You have an exceptional ability to focus your attention.
- You can be so focused that you forget your surroundings or to take care of yourself.
- You enjoy spending time with people who have intelligence and interests you respect.
- You're full of knowledge, ideas, and opinions.
- You want to find someone to connect with but are afraid of losing your self-reliance.
- You fear you aren't equipped to face life, so you prefer to retreat into your mind.
- You're not comfortable dealing with your own emotions.
- You are shy, non-intrusive, independent, and reluctant to seek help.
- You're not usually comfortable with your social skills.
- When you make friends, you are devoted, and form lifelong attachments.
- You rarely or never experience boredom.

If you can relate to more than half of the above statements, you're probably a Five or you have a strong Five wing. Keep reading to learn more about your type!

Core Belief

The belief driving your behavior is that you must protect yourself from a world that gives too little and demands too much. Your unconscious fear is that there may not be enough resources for everyone to survive. You seek self-sufficiency and make few demands on others. You withdraw into your private world of thought to protect yourself from the world. By not making demands, you feel as if you are conserving resources and guaranteeing your own survival.

Avoidance: *Scarcity and Intrusion*

You fear and avoid intrusion of others who might make demands on your resources and energy. Your privacy, vast accumulation of knowledge and self-sufficiency protect you from expending too much of your energy. You fear you are not well-equipped for life, so you avoid intrusion of others so your inadequacy will not be exposed.

Trap: *Detaching to Study*

You enjoy escaping into your own mind and accumulating knowledge. You seek to build your confidence and ability to face the world through your intelligence. However, this habit can become so all-consuming that you neglect your emotional health and relationships.

Idealization: *I am wise and competent.*

You focus your energy on projecting the image that you are knowledgeable. You feel that knowledge is scarce and extremely valuable, so you equip yourself with as much of it as possible to survive.

Defense Mechanism: *Isolation*

Through isolation, you avoid feeling overwhelmed and empty. You retreat into your mind as a way of cutting yourself off from feelings. You may also isolate different parts of your life, such as keeping your work life entirely separate from your personal life. You may separate relationships so that your friends never meet each other. The purpose of all this isolation is to eliminate the risk of being exposed as inadequate and ill-equipped for life.

Passion: *Avarice (Hoarding)*

Although you appear intellectually competent, you lack confidence in yourself. You feel other people's demands might be too much for you and you won't be able to meet them. You "hoard" your time and energy by keeping as much of it to yourself as possible because you feel that you will not be enough to meet the needs of others.

Description

You value knowledge, understanding, and insight highly and you view your journey as one of constant learning. Your learning is mainly observational, and you seek to gain as much knowledge as possible about particular subjects.

Many, like you, have made significant discoveries and advances in various fields; at your best, you are brilliantly innovative! Your powers of observation, perception, and concentration are remarkable. Your active mind keeps you from ever being bored.

You take pride in being self-sufficient; by not depending on anyone or having anyone depend on you, you feel you are conserving what little resources you might have for making it through this life. As a member of the *Thinking Triad*, you deal with anxiety. Your anxiety is about your ability to face the outside world, and you cope with it by withdrawing and attempting to gain enough knowledge to become competent.

Although you isolate, you still sometimes crave the company of others. You make excellent company for those who are interested in your knowledge. Others find you a bit odd but interesting. Sometimes, you resemble the image of the "absent-minded professor" who is so caught up in his own studies and thoughts that he forgets to feed himself, is late for meetings, and doesn't hear the phone ring.

Directions of Integration and Disintegration

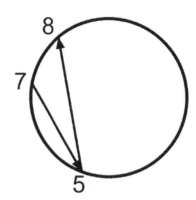

Your direction of integration is Eight, the Challenger. When you are emotionally healthy, you resemble a healthy Eight. When you see that your isolation is harmful to your psychological health, you try making more contact with yourself and others. As you become more in tune with yourself and reality, you will display the qualities of a good leader (a healthy Eight). You find you can help others with your expertise.

If you are less healthy but still secure, you look like an average Eight. When you are feeling sure of yourself, you assert your boundaries more aggressively, possibly becoming confrontational and controlling.

Your direction of disintegration is type Seven, the Enthusiast. You react to stress by isolating, but eventually, you start to need some interaction with others. Nervous energy builds up in you so that you become restless and anxious. Your behavior becomes erratic and impulsive, and you may become very talkative.

Levels of Development

The following is a very brief breakdown of your levels of development as a Five, so you can begin to recognize your psychological health and warning signs of emotional deterioration:

- **Healthy**
    - **Level 1 (at your best):** Your self-image is not attached to your knowledge. You are wise, connected to your environment, and participate in life. You become a visionary and make exciting new discoveries.
    - **Level 2:** You are fascinated by observing life. You notice everything, concentrate fully, and remain mentally alert.

- o **Level 3:** You are an expert field. You are very independent and somewhat quirky.

- **Average**
  - o **Level 4:** You study and think extensively before acting. You are very intellectual and specialized in your knowledge.
  - o **Level 5:** You spend a lot of time escaping into your thoughts and detaching from reality. Your strongest interests may be strange or disturbing.
  - o **Level 6**: You resent anyone and anything that intrudes on your isolation and study time. You are purposefully argumentative and antagonistic.

- **Unhealthy**
  - o **Level 7:** You grow radically isolated and eccentric. You are emotionally unstable and antisocial.
  - o **Level 8:** You become obsessed with disturbing ideas which fascinate and disturb you at the same time. At this point, you are delusional.
  - o **Level 9:** You are so out of touch with reality that you may become self-destructive and deranged. Possibly Schizoid Avoidant or Schizotypal personality disorder.

Subtypes/Instincts

If you are a *social* Five, you are more outgoing than most other Fives. Your comfort in social situations depends on having some area of expertise to talk about or some skill to demonstrate. You may look down on those around you, feeling that they might not be able to understand your superior intelligence.

As a *sexual* Five, you desire intimacy and connection than most other Fives. This conflicts with your impulse to withdraw and isolate, so you are cautious and selective about who you get close to. You believe others will find you odd or even disturbing. Your desire is to find someone to share your private world of knowledge while helping you survive the life for which you feel ill-equipped.

Finally, if you are a *self-preservation* Five, you can be the most isolated. You are extremely private and withdrawn, but you do not focus on accumulating physical comforts. You spend a great amount of time alone, but you may socialize with a few people that you trust. If you do not live alone, you need some special place that is your own, where no one can intrude upon your solace.

Psychological and Spiritual Growth

Your growth as a Five takes place when you start putting yourself in the world. You believed you would gain confidence from studying, but it comes from experience. If you practice being present in your physical body and emotions instead of retreating to your mind, you will become more grounded and balanced. You have been denying that you even have emotions, but you feel things deeply. You need to learn how to experience those emotions at the moment and express them as they come.

When you feel the urge to withdraw and isolate, try to stay connected for just a little longer before retreating. Gradually allow more people into the circle of those you trust and practice talking about personal matters to those people. When you are with acquaintances outside of your circle of friends, try sharing something you wouldn't normally share. Pay attention to how long you talk – you may tend to talk too little or too long. Watch your audience for cues to see if you should talk more or less. Are they bored? Interested? Wanting to hear more? It may help to observe the interactions between other people to pick up on conversational skills.

There is more to you than your mind. Get in touch with your body by taking up some kind of physical activity. This could be anything from intense exercise to cooking or knitting. Try engaging in physical activities with friends or family.

You have been conserving your time and energy for fear of not having enough to go around, but you can now try to share with others. If you see an opportunity to be of service and want to help, give it a try. You may find that you feel more connected to the human race and more fulfilled as a result.

Because you have suppressed parts of yourself for so long, you may even want to seek expert help with getting in touch with your emotional and physical self. In the chapter about Type Nine, the Peacemaker, we mentioned bioenergetic work, which can also be helpful for Fives.

In describing his experience of learning from the Enneagram, one Five proclaims that bioenergetic work truly helped him to get in touch with his emotions. His instructor kept up a conversation with him while he engaged in the physical work of the session. When this Five experienced intense emotion during the session, the instructor had him strike a pillow with a tennis racquet! This technique proved very effective, allowing him to release his control over his emotions and let them come out.

This Five explains that, after this session, he realized how much pent-up rage and fear he had never recognized within himself. Once he became aware of his hidden emotions, he said that they no longer had the power to control him.

If you are a Five who struggles with the concept of being in touch with your emotions, you can find help also. There are many possible ways for you to accomplish this, including bioenergetic work. The important thing is for you to realize that you can start to feel more whole by getting in touch with your emotions and staying grounded in the world instead of retreating from it.

Relationships

This final section consists of lists with helpful hints *for* Fives in relationships and for people in relationships *with* Fives. These include business relationships, romantic relationships, and parent-child relationships.

Business Relationships FOR *Fives:*
- Try sharing and giving more of yourself, while taking in more support from others.
- When you feel the need to talk endlessly on a subject, pause and wait to see if anyone expresses interest in that subject.
- Know if you are just using your knowledge just to impress people.
- Bring your mind to the present by having a watch that beeps hourly. Be productive and be aware always of the present.
- Pay attention to the contributions of others and let them know when they are appreciated.
- Try reaching out to someone at work that is struggling, even if this makes you uncomfortable at first.

Business Relationships WITH *Fives:*
- Approach them slowly and thoughtfully.
- Value knowledge and talk about ideas together.
- Give them time to think things over; don't pressure them to make decisions immediately.
- Ask them to directly communicate with you and don't just assume.
- When conflicts arise, agree to disagree if possible.
- Challenge them to stay present when they want to withdraw.
- Give them a lot of information.

Parenting FOR *Fives:*
- You are likely good, very perceptive, kind, and devoted to your child. Keep it up!
- Avoid being over-demanding. Set fair expectations and communicate with them clearly.
- Research what is developmentally appropriate for your child's intellectual progress; do not expect too much from them.
- Allow your child to express strong emotions. Ask them to explain how they feel and why, if they are able.
- If your child is not a Five, you can still encourage them to read and learn about subjects that interest them.

Parenting When Your CHILD *Is A Five*
- They may spend a lot of time alone reading or making collections; take an interest in these hobbies with them.
- Let them know when you are proud of their achievements.
- Encourage them to get involved in events rather than just observing.

- When they look calm, they may be hiding anxiety. Don't assume they are fine just because they are not expressing emotions.
- Respect their need for alone time but set expectations for how much time they spend interacting with you and the family.
- They are sensitive and avoid conflict. Ask them regularly how they feel about different situations and people.

Romantic Relationships FOR *Fives:*
- Practice revealing personal matters and feelings to your partner. Ask them for patience and sympathy as you learn this new skill.
- If you feel the urge to withdraw because your partner is expressing emotions, stand your ground and practice deep breathing while remaining present and listening.
- Include the setting of limits and ask for what you want.
- Let them know what you value about them.
- Share equal time with them in conversation instead of monopolizing the time by talking about your areas of expertise.
- Spend time in some kind of physical activity together.

Romantic Relationships WITH *Fives:*
- Giving and respecting their alone time is not a rejection.
- Assure them that they can safely share their personal experiences and feelings by giving them the time and space they need to do so.
- Don't pressure them for fast decisions or immediate contact.
- Let them communicate with you directly and don't make assumptions.
- Learn a little about their areas of expertise so you can participate in conversations about these.
- Be independent, not clingy.
- Speak in a straightforward manner.
- If they seem aloof or distant, they may be feeling uncomfortable.
- Support them in situations when they are extremely uncomfortable. For example, help them to endure a short time at a big party and then gracefully take your leave together.
- Take time to vocally appreciate their gifts of observation, perception, and focus.

Chapter 11: Type 6 – The Loyalist

Type 6 Checklist: *Ask yourself if the following statements are true for you.*

- You are meticulous, disciplined, and persevering.
- You have a talent for seeing potential problems and dealing with them before they get out of hand.
- You enjoy being of service and want to contribute to the world.
- You are good at heading up projects because you can organize resources and prioritize tasks well.
- You struggle with doubt and anxiety, usually finding plenty to worry about.
- Sometimes, you test people by provoking them to see how they will react.
- You are slow and cautious to commit, but once you do commit, you are loyal to a fault.
- You do not trust people quickly.
- You often do not have much faith in yourself.
- You prefer having a predictable environment.
- You often feel like you are looking for something or someone to believe in.
- You may complain about stress, but you thrive on it.
- You can be very stable, self-reliant, and courageous.
- You fear to be without support and guidance.
- You are fiercely loyal to ideas, systems, and beliefs that have proven themselves to you.

If you can relate to more than half of the above statements, chances are that you are a Six or you have a strong Six wing. Keep reading to learn more about your type!

Core Belief

The central belief that drives your behavior is that the world is a dangerous and threatening place. You believe that you need to be prepared and loyal so that people can count on you. You feel that not everyone can be trusted, and you cannot let your guard down. At the same time, you believe that you should not show any fear.

Avoidance: *Uncertainty, Vulnerability, and Deviance (from Group Norms)*

You have many inner anxieties and you try to calm them by trying to make your world predictable and trouble-free, even though this is impossible. Once you have found a group to be loyal to, you avoid any appearance of disloyalty such as deviating from the group norms.

Trap: *Creating Safety and Security*

You compulsively try to create a feeling of security through meticulous planning, attempts to anticipate problems, and distrusting people until they have proven themselves to you. Once you have committed to something or someone, you remain committed to a fault because you feel secure in that commitment. To detach would disrupt the safety that you treasure.

Idealization: *I am loyal.*

You want the people in your trusted circle to know they can count on you to guard their safety no matter what, even though you feel deep anxiety within yourself. You cultivate this image by trying to constantly be prepared for any eventuality.

Defense Mechanism: *Projection*

Projection is a method of attributing things to others that you cannot accept about yourself. If you think negatively about a friend but cannot admit it, you may accuse someone else of thinking negatively about them. Your projection is so thorough that you often imagine it to be true.

Passion: *Anxiety*

As a member of the *Thinking Triad*, your central emotional issue is anxiety. Your struggle with anxiety is much more central than types Five and Seven. You are continually on the look-out for dangers or problems and are particularly talented at imagining worst-case scenarios. Even though you try to be prepared for any scenario, your anxiety may be so extreme that you are too fearful to truly be prepared.

Brief Description

Your type has been called The Guardian, The Devil's Advocate, The Skeptic, The Questioner, or The Loyalist. You may like to believe you are realistic, but others think you are pessimistic.

Although it takes you a while to trust a person or organization, you are extremely loyal to them once they have proven themselves. You are loyal to the extent that you might hang on to people, beliefs, and groups much longer than they deserve. You fear to let go of them because you feel that you will not have support or guidance without them.

You have been accused of "overthinking" life issues. You second-guess yourself regularly and have trouble trusting your own thinking and judgments. You may have tremendous difficulty making big decisions, but you do not want anyone else to make those decisions for you either.

Some of your strengths are your ability to plan, attention to detail, courage, and preparedness. You are devoted to your values and very team-oriented. These qualities make you a valued contributor in many work environments. When emotionally healthy, you trust your inner instincts and you have the potential to be a powerful influence for worthy causes.

One thing that sets your type apart from others is that you seem to be a bundle of contradicting traits. You are simultaneously weak and strong, courageous and fearful, doubter and believer, passive and aggressive, and so on. When it comes to your issues with fear or anxiety, your response may be to surrender to the self-doubt or to confront it head-on. This unpredictability can be especially confusing to people who are close to you.

Directions of Integration and Disintegration

Your direction of integration is towards type Nine, the Peacemaker. This means that when you are emotionally healthy, you take on some of the characteristics of a healthy Nine. If you learn to trust yourself, you can relax and accept life circumstances without anxiety. You find that you can support other people because you are not doubtful of your own security anymore. You find inner quiet when you stop second-guessing yourself.

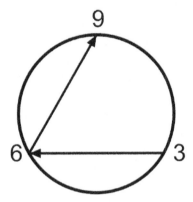

If you are less emotionally healthy but still, in secure conditions, you may display the traits of an average Nine, who deals with stress by shutting down and disengaging from life. In this state, you may prefer to numb yourself to life's stresses with comfortable routines.

Your direction of disintegration is toward type Three, the Achiever. Your first reaction to stress is to become extremely anxious but when stress is excessive, you leap into a mode of hyper-productivity. You try to deal with your anxieties and feelings of inadequacy by working hard and constantly getting things done. You may become so task-oriented that you damage relationships.

Levels of Development

The following is a very brief breakdown of your levels of development as a Six, so you can begin to recognize your psychological health and warning signs that you may have some work to do.

- **Healthy**
    - **Level 1 (at your best):** You find guidance within yourself and trust that you are secure. You are genuinely trustworthy and able to provide support and true emotional bonds.
    - **Level 2:** You are lovable and affectionate. You value trust and forming permanent relationships/alliances with others.
    - **Level 3:** You are responsible and reliable. You work hard to create security and stability in your world. You are dedicated to community causes that you believe in.

- **Average**
    - **Level 4:** You invest your energy in anything you think will bring you stability. You are constantly on the look-out for problems. You look outside yourself for safety.
    - **Level 5:** Your anxiety causes you to be reactive and pessimistic. You have trouble making decisions and are often too cautious to take any action. Your uncertainty makes you unpredictable.
    - **Level 6:** Your deep insecurities cause you to become defensive and blame others for your problems. You are controlling and suspicious, dealing with your fears by trying to instill them in others.

- **Unhealthy**
    - **Level 7:** You fear that your security is gone, so you begin to panic and seek safety elsewhere. Your feelings of inferiority cause you to belittle others and cause divisions.
    - **Level 8:** You become paranoid that others are out to get you. You act irrationally and potentially violent.
    - **Level 9:** You reach a level of hysteria and become self-destructive through suicidal ideations or addictive substances. Possible Passive-Aggressive or Paranoid personality disorders.

Subtypes/Instincts

If your dominant instinct is *social*, you look for security in your social connections. You make yourself valuable to a group by devoting your time and energy to it. By ingratiating yourself to a social circle, you hope to find the sense of security that you crave. You want others to see you as approachable and safe.

If you are a Six whose dominant instinct is *sexual*, you look for safety in your bond with a partner. You are emotionally intense because you are anxious about your ability to choose and keep the right mate, and because you have trouble trusting that your significant other will really be there for you. You feel the need to prove your desirability so that your mate will continue to find you attractive. Under stressful conditions, you may experience strong shifts in your feelings toward your partner.

Finally, if you are a Six who values *self-preservation* as your dominant instinct, you focus on protecting your physical resources, like money and food. You feel more secure when you are the one in charge of financial decisions, and you have trouble trusting other people to be responsible. You are more introverted than other Sixes. To protect your sense of security, you might stay in bad situations (like abusive relationships) longer than you should.

Psychological and Spiritual Growth

Your growth as a Six happens when you recognize that your security must come from within. There is no external relationship, structure, organization, or idea that will continually work to provide you with the sense of safety that you so desperately desire. You must learn to trust your instincts and ability to make decisions. This may take a lot of time and effort, but the reward of finding faith in yourself will be worth it.

You may think that you have more anxieties than most, but everyone experiences anxieties. When you are fearful, learn to recognize it and understand it instead of working frantically to alleviate it. Try learning a few calming breathing exercises.

Take a moment to think on your past anxieties and realize that few to none of your feared worst-case scenarios have ever come true. When you focus on the negative things that might happen, you only weaken yourself. Choose to strengthen yourself by focusing on the positive.

Try to trust people more freely and turn to them when you need help or a listening ear. You fear rejection, but it's important that you try to find someone trustworthy and allow yourself to get close to them. You have been desiring closer relationships but are fearful that people think badly of you. The truth is that most people probably think better of you than you realize.

One Six explains how she benefitted from Enneagram teachings and from learning how to do breathing exercises. Before, her fear of being hurt made her put up barriers. Rather than expressing any feelings, she kept other people out, telling herself that they couldn't be trusted. She was afraid of revealing much about herself because she thought people might use that information against her.

Because she wanted to experience a fuller life, she decided to learn of the Enneagram and breath work. Instead of being defensive all the time, she learned to soften her core. Breathing techniques helped her to sense her feelings and work out her aggression. She found that she could feel love along with other emotions and that she could let go of her suspicion towards others. She was relieved to discover that she was better able to relate to other people once she was more in touch with her inner self.

If you are a Six who has let your distrust of others keep you from them, there is hope for you. Breathing exercises can be one key to unlocking your inner self and finding the close relationships that you desire and deserve. Learn to trust and rely on others, and you will reap great rewards.

Relationships

This final section consists of lists with helpful hints *for* Sixes in relationships and for people in relationships *with* Sixes. These include business relationships, romantic relationships, and parent-child relationships.

Business Relationships FOR *Sixes:*
- Try balancing the negative spin you tend to put on situations with positives.
- Put your skills to good use by heading up projects, prioritizing tasks, and organizing details.
- Welcome tasks and situations that cause anxiety and move ahead into them. Focus on breathing through the fear.
- Instead of distrusting people until they prove themselves trustworthy, try trusting them until they prove themselves untrustworthy.
- Recognize your own concerns and emotions instead of projecting them on others.

Business Relationships WITH *Sixes:*
- Value their problem-solving skills; their attention to problems; come to an agreement on procedures and rules.
- Avoid changing the rules abruptly or withholding information.
- Try not to tell them their concerns are unfounded.
- Together, acknowledge the possibilities of things going wrong before you move ahead.
- When you sense conflict, don't be ambiguous. Show your cards as much as possible.
- Challenge them to take responsibility for their reactions instead of blaming external reasons.
- When possible, get them to see the humor in situations.

Parenting FOR *Sixes:*
- You are likely very loving and nurturing. Keep it up!
- You might be reluctant to give your child independence. Try to let go in stages, explaining your trust in them and your expectations a little at a time.
- Try not to be consumed with worry over your child's well-being. Do all you can to care for them and teach them to be safe, then let go of your worry. You cannot control what happens to them every hour of the day, and bad things could happen with or without your worry.
- Work on setting boundaries and saying no when necessary. Your child will still love and respect you, and your secure bond will still be intact.

Parenting When Your CHILD *Is A Six*
- They may be over-anxious and hypervigilant. Try to help them alleviate their fears by talking about them.
- Assure them that they can trust you, but also train them to know what to do in case of emergency.
- Don't get in battles in which they might see you as the enemy. Instead, explain that your rules and expectations are there to protect them and help them grow into a confident and competent adult.
- Do your best to avoid unpredictability in the home. Provide a safe and nurturing environment in which they don't find excessive reasons for their anxiety.

Romantic Relationships FOR *Sixes:*
- Resist the urge to become suspicious and controlling. If you suddenly find that you want to question your partner's trustworthiness, ask yourself what emotions you are not addressing.
- Work on trusting them steadfastly unless and until they give you reasons to doubt them.
- Before you overreact, try to pause to reflect on what you are feeling and what prompted that emotion.
- Be aware of your pessimism, because it causes you to project negativity on your significant other.
- Learn to stay in the present moment with your partner.
- Discuss your insecurities instead of internalizing them and allowing them to change your attitudes and behavior.

Romantic Relationships WITH *Sixes:*
- Help them to face their fears directly.
- Carefully listen to them and be clear and direct.
- Anxiety doesn't define them, so don't judge them by just that.
- Reassure them that everything is ok between the two of you.
- Gently encourage them to try new experiences.
- When possible, try to lighten the mood by making jokes and laughing with them, not at them.
- Tell them you appreciate their commitment to you and others.
- Try spontaneous reassurances, romance, and occasional surprises.
- When they identify problem areas, don't argue with them. Recognize the issue. Even if you aren't ready to discuss it further, let them know you are committed to talking it through soon.
- Remind them that they are valuable to you.

Chapter 12: Type 7 – The Enthusiast

Type 7 Checklist: *Ask yourself if the following statements are true for you.*

- You are energetic and like to make a lot of plans.
- You don't see the point of denying yourself anything you enjoy.
- You are entrepreneurial and skilled at networking and self-promotion.
- If you focus your many talents and put your mind to something, you can be very successful.
- You have trouble focusing because you believe that something better might be waiting for you.
- You're afraid that everyone will find out that deep down, you feel empty inside.
- You like to keep your options open.
- You have a hard time empathizing with people in emotional pain.
- You are curious and adventurous.
- You tend to focus your energy on maintaining your freedom and happiness.
- You dislike feeling trapped or limited by having few options.
- You love to fill up your social calendar.
- You can be very creative.
- You bounce back quickly from setbacks and disappointments.
- You are often very slow to make commitments to people.

If you can relate to more than half of the above statements, you are probably a Seven or you have a strong Seven wing. Keep reading to learn more about your type!

Core Belief

The belief that drives your behavior is that the world limits and frustrates people and causes pain that you can escape by staying upbeat and keeping your possibilities open.

Avoidance: *Pain*

You flee from the emotional pain of the world by engaging in as many distractions and activities as possible.

Trap: *Imagining and Planning*

You can get so caught up in planning the next adventure or party that you never actually live in the moment or take the time to be aware of how you are feeling.

Idealization: *I am OK.*

You want everyone around you to believe that you are feeling great and having the time of your life, even though you may be hiding feelings of loneliness and emptiness. You may not even be aware of your inner pain.

Defense Mechanism: *Rationalization*

Through rationalization, you reframe negative experiences in a positive light. To help maintain the pretense of you being okay and prevent suffering, you are doing this reframing.

Passion: *Gluttony*

Because you constantly hide painful feelings that you aren't willing to acknowledge, you may seek constant stimulation to distract yourself. You greedily devour every experience you encounter. You never fully enjoy anything because you are always looking forward to the next thing.

Description

Your type has been called The Generalist, The Visionary, The Adventurer, The Epicure, or The Enthusiast. You constantly look at the bright side of everything, and your optimism draws other people to you. You are enthusiastic about almost everything that catches your attention, and you approach life with curiosity, optimism, and an adventurous spirit. You pursue what you want in life with cheerful determination.

Besides optimism, your strengths include a quick mind and the ability to pick up new information and skills quickly. These are great advantages but also make it difficult for you to decide what to do with yourself. Because learning comes easily to you, you may not appreciate your abilities as much as if you had to struggle to obtain them.

As a member of the *Thinking Triad*, your emotional issues center on anxiety, although this may not be as apparent as for Fives and Sixes. You are out of touch with your inner guidance; consequently, you doubt your ability to make decisions. You cope with this anxiety by keeping your mind excessively busy and by continually moving from one experience to the next.

At your core, you fear that you may not be able to find what you really want out of life. This fear prompts you to try everything, either to find what you want or to "settle" for a substitute and create a little enjoyment along the way. You live to fulfill your desire for freedom and variety.

Wings

The personalities to either side of you on the Enneagram are Six, the Loyalist, and Eight, the Challenger. A Seven with a Six-Wing has been labeled "The Entertainer" by some, and a Seven with an Eight-Wing has been labeled "The Realist." Read the chapters on Six and Eight to decide if you identify with one of these wings.

Directions of Integration and Disintegration

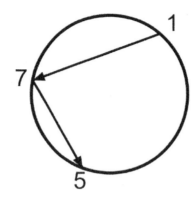

Your direction of integration is towards type Five, the Investigator. When you are emotionally healthy, you can resemble a healthy Five. If you learn to relax and tolerate uncomfortable feelings, you can focus more fully and use your gifts of creativity and insight. You become more productive by following your true interests.

If you are less emotionally healthy but still, in secure conditions, you may act like an average Five. When you get exhausted from all your adventurous Seven-ish tendencies, you might abruptly withdraw from your social life to rest and regroup.

Your direction of disintegration is towards type One, the Reformer. At times, you may feel frustrated that you are not accomplishing as much as you would like to because you have been jumping from one activity to another. When you feel this way, you act like an average One by trying to impose organization and control on yourself. This self-imposed order frustrates you more, and you become very critical with yourself and sometimes others.

Levels of Development

The following is a very brief breakdown of your levels of development as a Seven so you can begin to recognize your psychological health and warning signs of emotional deterioration.

- **Healthy**
    - **Level 1 (at your best):** You can live in each moment and enjoy each experience deeply. You have gratitude and appreciation for your blessings.
    - **Level 2:** You are cheerful, excitable, and enthusiastic about the experience. You very extroverted and spontaneous.
    - **Level 3:** You are multi-talented, productive, practical, and accomplished.

- **Average**
    - **Level 4:** You restlessly search for more options. You are adventurous but unfocused, trying to keep up with the latest trends.

- o **Level 5:** You are hyperactive, self-indulgent, and uninhibited. You have many ideas but rarely follow through.
- o **Level 6**: Your over-consumption reaches addictive levels. You are greedy and selfish, insensitive, demanding, and unsatisfied.

- **Unhealthy**
  - o **Level 7:** You fall prey to addictions in an effort to quiet your anxieties. You are childish and impulsive.
  - o **Level 8:** Your moods change erratically and you act compulsively. You essentially are in flight from yourself.
  - o **Level 9:** You have ruined your health and used up your energy. You may become claustrophobic and panicky. Corresponds to depression, suicidal tendencies, possible Bipolar disorder, and Histrionic personality disorder.

Subtypes/Instincts

If you recall from Chapter 2, each person is equipped with three basic instincts – social, sexual, and self-preservation. As a Seven, one of these three is your dominant instinct, and it uniquely influences your personality traits.

If you are a *social* Seven, you are extremely people-oriented, so your adventure planning is focused on group activities. You like looking to worthy causes to invest your creative energies on because you feel like you have the power to effect positive change in the world. You don't like committing to any particular person or cause because that makes you feel trapped. This commitment-phobia sometimes hurts the feelings of your friends.

As a *sexual* Seven, you bring your curiosity and adventurous spirit to relationships. You love getting intensely involved with new people and your magnetic personality makes it easy for you to capture their attention. You frustrate yourself and others, though, because you can quickly shift focus to another person, idea, or thing that seems more exciting.

Finally, if you are a *self-preservation* Seven, you enjoy material possessions. You spend a lot of time planning to buy or experience various luxury items. You are good at hunting down a good bargain, and you seek friends who share your interests. Sometimes, you have unrealistic expectations and can end up disappointed because the material world cannot always meet your needs.

Psychological and Spiritual Growth Recommendations

Your growth as a Seven depends on you realizing that you can find happiness in the present by being still and recognizing beauty all around you. When you stop focusing on the future and looking for bigger and brighter adventures, you will be able to live in the moment and deeply enjoy each experience, no matter how ordinary it may seem. Being open to the enjoyment of the here and now can also bring awareness of the spiritual life beyond what you can see, taste, and feel.

Begin by recognizing your impulses and letting them pass instead of giving in to them. This helps you focus on things that will benefit you on a deeper level. If you find you still feel that you must act on an impulse, try putting it off for a day and see if you still have the same desire tomorrow.

Try to choose on quality over quantity in your experiences and relationships. This can be learned by giving your full attention to each experience and person that you become involved with. Focus your attention on them instead of rushing on to something newer and seemingly shinier. Ask yourself if what you desire is what will be good for you in the long run.

Work on really listening to people so that you can fully appreciate what they are communicating to you. Make and fulfill commitments and learn to become more aware of others' feelings.

As much as you try to avoid negative feelings and experiences, you need to try to realize that it is limiting and damaging to only seek the positive. By allowing pain and uncomfortable emotions, you are opening yourself to the full human experience. You will be rewarded for your openness with a much deeper satisfaction in your existence.

You may be inspired by the experience of a Seven who learned where she could find true joy. She used to avoid pain at all possible costs, but she discovered the Enneagram during a time of great unavoidable pain. She began learning about how she had spent her life fleeing from discomfort, and she gained the courage to stay grounded even while she was experiencing pain.

This Seven learned how to make more rational life choices, instead of blindly following impulses that arose when she was trying to avoid difficult feelings. She has discovered that she is able to sit and feel her emotions and let them pass through her, no matter how long it takes.

She now knows that when she suddenly feels intensely euphoric, she needs to be careful and slow down. She is learning to be present in each moment, no matter how ordinary it may seem. She has benefited immensely from tai chi and mindfulness practices. This enlightened Seven says that she sometimes misses the euphoric highs of being an unfettered Seven, but she has now found true joy and a sense of fulfillment in the here and now, thanks to her Enneagram work.

Take heart if you are a Seven who rushes from adventure to exhausting adventure in order to avoid feelings of pain and difficulty. You can also find lasting contentment in each moment as it passes if you take the time and do the work. You can learn to sit through your emotions, survive them and embrace them as a part of your true self.

Relationships

This final section consists of lists with helpful hints *for* Sevens in relationships and for people in relationships *with* Sevens. These include business relationships, romantic relationships, and parent-child relationships.

Business Relationships FOR *Sevens:*
- Work to focus on one task at a time.
- Fully listen to your coworkers and appreciate what they have to offer.
- Make an effort to stay the course with any idea or project you commit to.
- Try to adopt a realistic point of view. If something negative needs to be discussed, face it instead of avoiding it or reframing it.
- Calm your mind when you feel it racing ahead in a conversation or presentation.
- Use your optimism to the fullest by helping others see how they can learn from mistakes and setbacks.

Business Relationships WITH *Sevens:*
- Show appreciation for their stories and positive ideas.
- Don't be too negative. Also, don't insist to do a thing in just one way.
- Be with them while they're imagining new possibilities and having fun.
- When you sense conflict, challenge them to be responsible for the things they did wrong.
- Make them stop talking so that they can know what is needed from them by you or the other people.
- Encourage them in learning to calm their mind and be present in the moment.

Parenting FOR *Sevens:*
- You are good at helping children overcome challenges. Keep it up!
- Bring your creativity and sense of fun into your children's playtime. Help them foster their imagination.
- Try not to avoid the ordinary or negative so much that your children don't learn from their mistakes or grow up with unrealistic expectations from life.
- Don't over-commit. Only promise things that you can fulfill.
- Prioritize setting aside time for your children and don't violate that priority.
- Be mature in managing your disappointment if your family doesn't share your enthusiasm.
- Try to match your energy to that of your family.

Parenting When Your CHILD *Is A Seven*
- They are probably active and adventurous. Encourage these traits, but set boundaries.
- Help them rein in their excitement when it is inappropriate for a situation or place.
- Help them find activities where they can be around their peers.
- Encourage their imagination, but help them learn about focus and commitment by achieving one thing at a time and seeing projects through from beginning to end.

- Help them to appreciate the little things and point out the beauty of the ordinary things all around them.
- Applaud their optimism, but help them learn to express sadness and fear so they become comfortable with these feelings.

Romantic Relationships FOR *Sevens:*
- Learn to be present at the moment with your mate.
- Practice fully listening to what they have to say.
- When you feel boxed in and tempted to look for a shiny, new relationship, pause to remember all the wonderful things about who you are with now.
- When you feel hurt or confused, acknowledge it and don't try to reframe it in a positive light. Talk about it if you can.
- Appreciate the joy and beauty in day-to-day life with your significant other.
- Try to take any criticism as constructive, if it is intended in that way. Ask for clarification if necessary.

Romantic Relationships WITH *Sevens:*
- Know that you might feel either adored or ignored from moment to moment. Express why you are feeling that way.
- Be kind and gentle with any criticism. State the good news before the bad.
- Know that they are out of touch with negative emotions, and help them practice expressing them.
- Join them in enjoying creativity and planning fun adventures.
- Help them commit to projects or plans and see them through to the end.
- When they express boredom, know that they may be masking other feelings that are uncomfortable. Help them get in touch with these.
- Use kindness and thoughtfulness to help them express avoided emotions.
- Help them focus on realistic plans and staying in (and appreciating) the present.

Conclusion

Thank you for making it through to the end of *Enneagram Made Easy*. Let's hope it was informative and able to provide you with all of the tools you need to achieve your goals, whatever they may be.

The next step is to keep learning and growing! On the next page, we have included a helpful list of websites that are literal fonts of information on Enneagram-based learning and growth. Through these, you can delve further into any Enneagram-related topics that you wish to pursue. You'll find more tests to confirm your basic personality type. You will discover a dearth of information about various Enneagram types in relationships and in the business world. You will read about other enthusiasts' personal experiences of growth and self-discovery. You will find more suggestions for growth, meditations, and physical exercises that will benefit your personality type. You can find others seeking to learn more and find out where workshops and classes near you may be hosted. In online forums, you can find others of your type and begin communicating with each other. Our hope is that this book is just the beginning of your Enneagram journey to wholeness and spiritual health.

Finally, if you found this book useful in any way, a review is always appreciated!

One last thing before you go – Can I ask a small favor? I need your help! If this book has been helpful to you, could you share your experience by providing an honest feedback and review? This wouldn't take much of your time (a sentence will be very much appreciated), but a massive help for me and absolutely good Karma. **Due to not having the backing of a big publication I don't have the big reach or promotion to get my books out to a bigger audience and rely heavily on my readers help,** I take out time to read every review and I'm usually extremely excited for every honest feedback I get. If my book was able to inspire you, please express it! **This will help position me at the top for others seeking for new ideas and reasonable knowledge to access easily.**

I'm very grateful and I wish you every good things of life on your journey!

Warm regards,
Michael.

My Free Gift to You – Get One of My Audiobooks For Free!

If you've never created an account on Audible (the biggest audiobook store in the world), **you can claim one free audiobook of mine!** It's a simple process:

1. Pick one of audiobooks on Audible: https://www.audible.com/search?keywords=michael+wilkinson&ref=a_search_t1_header_search

2. Once you choose a book and open its detail page click the orange button "Free with 30-Day Trial Membership."

3. Follow the instructions to create your account and download you first free audiobook.

Not that you are NOT obligated to continue after your free trial expires. You can cancel you free trial easily anytime and won't be charged at all.

About The Author

Hello,

My name is Michael. My life has been one amazing and a passionate journey, which I feel want everyone to be a part of or experience in one way or the other. I'm someone who believes there is more to life than what we already know. I endeavored many things to transform my life way more than my expectations to a very fulfilling one, and it's time I shared with you this interesting journey in order for you to apply it, as well.

I was a shy and quiet kid and had the typical young life, growing up in England doing the normal kids things, playing football, video games and didn't know much of what I wanted in life except that I loved cartoons. That was until I turned 18 and started to explore the world. That changed the way I saw things and everything in life, it opened my eyes to what was possible. I became very eager to learn new things and explore more.

My interests include traveling, practicing martial arts, self-development, and offering value by assisting other people. I've got a keen passion for contents relating to sociology, mediation, social psychology, eastern philosophy, communication skills, emotional intelligence, NLP, time management, mindfulness, and relevant studies related to self-development and being the best version of whom you are.
Calm down, smile, and express the life inside of you... I look forward to hearing from you soon!

Helpful Resources

https://www.enneagraminstitute.com
- Official website of The Enneagram Institute.
- In-depth information about each of the 9 types.
- Purchase a longer test to confirm your type.
- Learn more about relationships between different types.
- Find out about Enneagram workshops and other training.

https://www.enneagramworldwide.com
- Offers a structured curriculum for your personal development.
- Exploration through listening to personal experiences of others.
- Comparisons between Enneagram types.
- Description of instinctual subtypes.
- Further insight into applying the Enneagram to your life.

https://www.integrative9.com
- Uses the Enneagram to provide development solutions for individuals, teams, and organizations.
- Information and products about each of the 9 types as well as the subtypes.
- Specializes in products for organizations and teams.
- Worldwide training and events.

https://theenneagramatwork.com
- Features products and workshops geared toward individuals, businesses, and organizations.
- Information about Enneagram coaching and typing.
- In-depth articles on various Enneagram topics.
- Information about Enneagram types in the workplace, on teams, and as leaders.

https://www.9types.com
- Diagrams that illustrate the key motivations and behaviors of each type.
- In-depth looks at each type through the lenses of several important sources.
- Information on all possible combinations of romantic relationships between Enneagram types.

http://drdaviddaniels.com/the-enneagram/
- Recent and relevant Enneagram Blog topics.
- Registration for weekly reflections.
- Links to podcasts and videos.
- In-depth information about relationships for each type.
- Growth recommendations for each type.

http://www.enneagram-monthly.com
- A journal dedicated to Enneagram discussion and education.
- Narratives by and about each type.
- Link for subscribing to the full journal.

http://theenneagraminbusiness.com
- E-learning, resources and professional services geared towards learning about Enneagram types in organizations.

- Access consulting tools, training, coaching and retreats.
- Useful information about each Enneagram type in various roles of the business world.
- Certification programs, DVDs, etc. available in the store.

Source Materials

Acharya, S., & Shukla, S. (2012). Mirror neurons: Enigma of the metaphysical modular brain. *Journal of Natural Science, Biology and Medicine*, 118-124.

Barsade, S. G. (2002). The Ripple Effect: Emotional Contagion and its Influence on Group Behavior. *Administrative Science Quarterly*, 644-675.

Brown, L., Collins, N., Sangster, M.-D., Aron, A., Aron, E., & Acevedo, B. (2014). The highly sensitive brain: a fMRI study of sensory processing sensitivity and response to others' emotions. *Brain and Behavior*, 580-594.

Cloete, Dirk. "Explore the 9 Enneagram Type Descriptions." Integrative 9: Enneagram Solutions, 2018, www.integrative9.com/enneagram/introduction/.

"Enneagram Types." The Narrative Enneagram, 2018, www.enneagramworldwide.com/tour-the-nine-types/.

Iacoboni, M. (2009). Imitation, Empathy, and Mirror Neurons. *Annual Reviews of Psychology*, 653-670.

McCraty, R., Atkinson, M., Tomasino, D., & Tiller, W. (1998). The Electricity of Touch: Detection and Measurement of Cardiac Energy Exchange Between People. *Research Library*.

O'Hanrahan, Peter. "Personal Stories." THE ENNEAGRAM AT WORK, 2018, theenneagramatwork.com/personal-stories/.

O'Hanrahan, Peter. "The Nine Enneagram Types." THE ENNEAGRAM AT WORK, 2018, theenneagramatwork.com/nine-enneagram-types/.

Riess, H. (2017). The Science of Empathy. *Journal of Patient Experience*, 74-77.

Riso, Don Richard., and Russ Hudson. Discovering Your Personality Type: the Essential Introduction to the Enneagram. Houghton Mifflin, 2003.

"The Nine Enneagram Type Descriptions." The Enneagram Institute, 2017, www.enneagraminstitute.com/type-descriptions/.

"Type Descriptions." 9types.Com, www.9types.com/descr/.

"Types." Enneagram Monthly, 2017, www.enneagram-monthly.com/types.html.

All images created by Rob Fitzel and used with permission from http://www.fitzel.ca/enneagram/graphics.html.

Made in the USA
Coppell, TX
07 December 2020